Benson J. Lossing and Historical Writing in the United States

Recent Titles in
Studies in Historiography

Ulrich Bonnell Phillips: A Southern Historian and His Critics
John David Smith

The People's Historian: John Richard Green and the Writing of
History in Victorian England
Anthony Brundage

The Inside of History: Jean Henri Merle d'Aubigné and Romantic
Historiography
John B. Roney

Benson J. Lossing and Historical Writing in the United States

1830–1890

Harold E. Mahan

Studies in Historiography, Number 4
John David Smith, Series Adviser

GREENWOOD PRESS
Westport, Connecticut • London

Library of Congress Cataloging-in-Publication Data

Mahan, Harold E.
   Benson J. Lossing and historical writing in the United States /
Harold E. Mahan.
      p.   cm.—(Studies in historiography, ISSN 1046–526X ; no. 4)
   Includes bibliographical references and index.
   ISBN 0–313–28806–2 (alk. paper)
      1. Lossing, Benson John, 1813–1891.   2. United States—
Historiography.   I. Title.   II. Series.
E175.5.L67M34   1996
973'.07202—dc20   95–35713

British Library Cataloguing in Publication Data is available.

Library of Congress Catalog Card Number: 95–35713
ISBN: 0–313–28806–2
ISSN: 1046–526X

First published in 1996

Greenwood Press, 88 Post Road West, Westport, CT 06881
An imprint of Greenwood Publishing Group, Inc.

Printed in the United States of America

CONTENTS

Benson J. Lossing
Courtesy of the State Historical Society of Wisconsin

Benson J. Lossing and Historical Writing in the United States

1

SCRIBBLERS AND SCHOLARS: AN INTRODUCTION

"There is a wide difference between *literary* and *intellectual* distinction. A mere scribbler who is fortunate in hitting on a popular subject at a proper time, may attain to a wide literary distinction, while a stupendous mental organization and long and unintermitted studies are necessary to intellectual distinction."[1] The historical popularizer Benson J. Lossing (1813-1891), the subject of this study, had only recently begun his career when this comment appeared in the *Southern Literary Messenger*. Lossing may have never read it, but the contrast the *Messenger* made between scribblers and scholars held much significance for his career.

Most importantly, these words reflected the contrasts with which many nineteenth-century writers of American history wrestled. Did the scribbler/scholar contrast hold validity? If so, how much? Could writers attain intellectual distinction in some works, even if in other writings they set their sights lower? Who, after all, decided which authors resided in each category: publishers, readers, reviewers, or one's peers? Or did the categories represent contested ground for all groups active in creating and dissimulating historical literature?

This study explores these questions in the context of Lossing's career and the role of historical writing in shaping and reflecting nineteenth-century American culture. But even at the outset, we can suggest tentative answers. Lossing's relationship to the *Messenger's* categories was complex, as his status as either a scribbler or a scholar often shifted, many times for no obvious or simple reason.

Although Lossing enjoyed national fame after 1850, he never rested on his laurels. Both a love of work and financial pressure prodded him to write more and more throughout his life. Often Lossing's writings did not offer notable historical insight. He did produce some works that contained intelligent, accurate narratives and reflected careful research. But he had to keep writing partly because his best books did not always reward him or his publishers with commercial success.

Whatever his gifts as a writer and researcher, Lossing often committed egregious errors in his business dealings. As a young man, he tried to edit two newspapers at once, until he had to suspend one when the work proved unbearable. He transferred publication rights for his vast Civil War *Pictorial History* from one firm to another, then watched the work's market disappear. A three-volume Centennial history sold 70,000 copies; but before publication Lossing declined a royalty agreement and simply took a lump sum for his work. Arguably, as far as commercial savvy went, Lossing did not behave even like an intelligent scribbler. Yet even contemporaries who did not value his influence admitted that he did make a significant impact on Americans' perceptions of their national past.

One reviewer made that point succinctly: "[n]o writer has done more to popularize the history of his own country than Mr. Lossing."[2] When librarian William F. Poole made this comment, he was not complimenting Lossing. For Poole, Lossing's proclivity for uncritical thinking had burdened the nation's historical consciousness with layers of distortion and legend. More rigorous investigators must now labor to give Americans a more accurate vision of their past. But Poole harbored fears that this demythologizing effort might prove unavailing with most Americans. In his view, Lossing and similar writers had left indelible marks on many readers' awareness of past events and the relationship of those events to their lives.

Poole's argument contains much truth. Over a fifty-year career of historical writing, Lossing proved himself capable of naive credulity in weighing evidence, and of snap judgments and stubborn prejudices in evaluating historical actors' motivations. In Lossing's hand, history often embodied no more than "tales generally agreed upon." Even worse for academicians, Lossing worked feverishly to gain advantage from topics that promised wider sales; in this sense he was essentially a "historian on the make." During Lossing's life, such criticisms usually took muted form; but they surfaced nonetheless. In 1874 one antiquarian, as another party recorded, "expressed great contempt for Lossing as a historian, considering him a mere hack—besides being credulous & even reckless about facts."[3]

But such critiques told only part of Lossing's story. His best books—especially the *Pictorial Field-Book of the Revolution* (1850-1852 and later editions) and a similar work on the War of 1812—displayed stylistic lucidity and depth of research that readers found astonishing.[4] Lossing also held a solid reputation among other historians. One thought that, in contrast to Washington Irving, Lossing did a good job citing his sources and acknowledging indebtedness to other researchers. "You are a just, fair, honest man in all you do and all you have done; & no one, I am quite sure, stands higher in the regard of American scholars." "I wish you could hear all the kind words said of you a portion of which reaches my ears," another researcher commented in 1873. "You have invested History with a charm which has captivated many thousands of your countrymen to whom the study was before dry & repulsive and you have aroused and deepened the sentiment of patriotism in the hearts of myriads."[5]

Not all the compliments paid to Lossing were conscious or ever reached him. When the publisher of one historical book listed the best sources for endorsements, he remarked that "[w]e should have Parkman, Lossing & Bancroft by all means[.]" Lossing enjoyed noting that the New-York Historical Society reported its copy of one of his works as stolen three different times.[6] If one based a judgment of Lossing on his best work or his contemporary standing among his peers, we could ask why many scholars, both in his time and later, dismissed his achievements so easily.

But this study has wider goals than reviving Lossing's reputation or even tracing that reputation's history. Its aim is to assemble an intellectual biography of Lossing and to use his career to study how middle-class Americans of his time read, wrote, and thought about their nation's past. Such broad issues, as this statement implies—especially what we might characterize as "collective memory" or "the sociology of [historical] knowledge"—involve overlapping theoretical and methodological preconceptions that require some unpacking. In outlining these issues, we must suggest the far-reaching implications a study of historical ideas possesses for cultural history.

Humankind's gift or burden of memory affects most individuals and groups so profoundly that interpreting and reinterpreting events that we remember (or about which we learn and so remember indirectly) remains one of our fundamental tools for making sense of life and ourselves. All societies require some form(s) of historical consciousness to preserve the lessons and beliefs each generation inherits from its ancestors. In many ways, "culture" and "ideology" reflect people using past experience to understand and organize their present actions and relationships.[7]

The learning of these lessons is an open-ended process that unfolds differently among various societies and even for each individual.[8] But the idea that a "usable past" can aid the understanding of the present remains a conscious or unconscious goal for most individuals and groups. This was Carl Becker's point in his famous "Every Man His Own Historian" essay; but earlier observers anticipated Becker. In 1857, a clergyman expressed this thought when he quoted an anonymous source. "In a certain sense, all men are historians. Is not every memory written quite full with annals, wherein joy and mourning, conquest and loss, manifoldly alternate; and the whole fortunes of one little inward kingdom, and all its politics, foreign and domestic, stand ineffaceably recorded?"[9]

Recognizing the importance of collective memory to culture should encourage scholars to investigate how uses of the past have changed or showed continuity over time, and how these uses have related to social, political, and other issues. Thus a history of historical thought can advance some central aims of cultural history,[10] especially, in one scholar's words, "find[ing] those shared beliefs and assumptions and concerns that hold together the various groups and individuals and activities of a particular society."[11]

Still, the presence of several conceptual problems requires that historians of historical ideas maintain caution as they ask questions along these lines and seek materials that might answer them. A major difficulty is that although awareness of history seems to represent a fundamental component of any meaningful worldview, relatively few people express conscious thoughts about how they use perceptions of past events to make sense of their lives. This was even true in nineteenth-century America, when historical thought had relatively high standing as a cultural resource. Thus Lewis Saum's discussion of American thought in the 1850s could only present a few quotations from diaries that bore upon this issue.[12]

Saum's difficulty could offer any of several possible lessons. Perhaps people's habit of thinking about history is not, after all, very important for our understanding of culture and cultural history. At the other extreme, we might interpret the paucity of explicit sources to mean that an awareness of history was such a basic concept in nineteenth-century America that most individuals simply assumed it without examining its implications. This study avoids both of those explanations, contending instead that historical knowledge played a complex, multifaceted role in American culture, a role about which Americans themselves were in profound disagreement.

Many individuals of Lossing's time had little or no interest in studying history. As one observer commented, "[o]ther nations may glory in the Past, but we are the people of the Future."[13] Sometimes Americans expressed contempt for historical knowledge in general, as when one writer remarked that "[b]ut a small part of History is of essential interest. A great deal of it is no better than that 'the king of France with 30,000 men marched up the hill & then marched down again['.]"[14] Such attitudes troubled antiquarians who wanted to locate and preserve historical materials, usually from the Revolutionary period, they hoped would provide Americans with a usable past. It was with this group that Lossing, after searching for a historical topic that fit his gifts, cast his lot.[15]

This is not to say that only antiquarians cared about history; political theorists who felt a pressing need to relate past events (in particular the American Revolution and the 1787 Constitutional Convention) to contemporary issues also played a role in furthering national awareness of history. But another, and far larger, group included writers and publishers who had a direct material, as well as intellectual, stake in historical writing.

Ironically, given their concentration on the Revolutionary War, many of the arguments that antiquarians used in defending historical study sprang from British sources. One English essay that American publishers reprinted in the early 1800s presented a typical perspective with its assertion that history "is eminently productive of signal utility." This writer's comments paralleled traditions that had begun in Classical times, first because history offered so much "matter of warning and matter of instruction" to political leaders. Further, the writer characterized history as morally "extremely useful, as it points out the issues of things, and exhibits, as its general result, the reprobation consequent upon vice, and the glory which awaits virtue."[16] Nineteenth-century American historians repeatedly used such assumptions, finally making them such cliches that commentators felt little need to repeat or reevaluate them.[17]

Specifying which groups in nineteenth-century America displayed interest in history raises a particularly tortured methodological question for cultural historians: the meaning and status of "popular" culture.[18] In our case, can we identify a strata of "popular" historical literature for nineteenth-century America? The perspective underlying this study is that "popular," especially as one might apply it to American historiography in the 1800s, is not a helpful concept because it defies clear definition. This is mainly because "popular" possesses meaning only as we can contrast it with "elite" or "high" culture.[19] If we assume that "popular culture" has descriptive relevance for nineteenth-century historical thought and writing, the implication follows that the "high" historical literature that stands in contrast to that which was "popular" was more "professional" in possessing "scholarly" or "academic" qualities. Arguably this distinction makes sense for trends after 1880, when a self-conscious cadre of "professional" (in the limited but significant sense of "professional" meaning "academic") historians appeared.[20] But before that time, no academic historical profession existed in the United States. Hence for most of Lossing's life, this particular demarcation line possessed no meaning.

But might we still, even for the pre-1880 era, distinguish "scholarly" historians from those who wrote out of commercial motivations? Research and reflection suggests we cannot, at least not in any simple manner. The nineteenth-century American historians who typically and correctly receive most praise for scholarly prowess (George Bancroft, Francis Parkman, John L. Motley, and William H. Prescott) also sought to write lucidly and thus gain as wide a readership as possible, even if this meant relying on cheap editions. As Prescott remarked in 1858,

I should be very well content to exchange all the glories of typography . . . for the simpler styles of execution which would be like[ly] to introduce them to the acquaintance of a wider public. Independently of the money it would put into my pocket, I should feel that I had accomplished a nobler work if I could feel that it had become the household companion of the poor as well as the rich.[21]

The production of historical books sprang from complex and unstable mixtures of writers' and publishers' aims.

This complexity was evident in Lossing's career. Whether consciously or not, his writings grew out of both scholarly and money-making goals; often both were operative in the same projects. On one hand, some of his works leaned more toward scholarly exactitude (his editions of Revolutionary-era literature, for instance), while others made no such pretensions and sprang totally from commercial aims.[22] Hence Lossing himself probably believed there could be a tension between scholarship and popularity, although he did not think it true in every case. It was only in this limited sense that a "high/popular" distinction influenced Lossing's writing and marketing of his historical writings, and thereby played a role in his career.

A synopsis of the following chapters can help us grasp Lossing's career in historical writing and the ways its elements interrelate. This introductory section surveys Lossing's role in American culture and reasons for studying his career. Chapter 2 begins a narrative of his life through 1838, when he moved from Poughkeepsie to New York City. Lossing's up-and-down experiences in the metropolis serve as the focus for Chapters 3 and 4. Until 1848, Lossing displayed little promise of attaining fame as a historian; but then circumstances changed.

The Pictorial Field-Book of the Revolution, a vast travel-historical work that established Lossing's reputation, requires all of Chapter 5 for its analysis. Despite the *Field-Book*'s aclaim, its originator found no leisure after its publication. Through the 1850s, Lossing remained busy with various successful and (more often) failed projects; these supply the focus for Chapter 6. A polemic history of the Civil War and the reasons for its commercial failure are central to Chapter 7. By 1868, Lossing's career had reached a low ebb; but as he displayed twenty years earlier, he had a formidable capacity to rebound.

The work that most scholars view as Lossing's best, *The Pictorial Field-Book of the War of 1812* (1868), furnishes a major theme for Chapter 8, along with his writings during the 1876 Centennial of American independence. The ninth chapter traces the final decade of Lossing's life (1881-1891), and a concluding passage relates Lossing's career and legacies to trends in American historical writing in his and later times.

Lossing wrote or edited over fifty books, besides producing hundreds of periodical essays and editing several newspapers and magazines himself. I became familiar with all this material, but space limitations prohibit discussion of all his writings. Hence, for example, this study devotes little attention to Lossing's many school histories, and adult survey histories, or some biographical works. I have presented more discussion of works that displayed development in Lossing's thought (such as the periodicals he edited as a young man) or that had a noticeable impact on his career or contemporaries' interpretation of historical events (especially the *Field Books* on the American Revolution and the War of 1812, and the Civil War

Pictorial History).

One other aspect of this study requires comment. To limit repetitive references in the notes, for several works I have simply given volume and page references in parentheses within the text. This proved necessary, for instance, with the *Field-Book of the Revolution*, which defined Lossing's career, the 1812 *Field-Book*, and other volumes. My aim is to make both the notes and the general text more useful for readers.

Despite one commentator's assertion that Lossing was "more than a historian" because of his artistic and literary endeavors,[23] this study makes no pretension that Lossing was a great scholar. He was a consistent but often unimaginative and self-satisfied exponent of what Herbert Butterfield called "the Whig Interpretation of History," a perspective that viewed all past development as leading naturally and inevitably to the glories of American society dominated by people like himself.[24] Apart from the *Field-Books*, one could argue that his years of hard work produced mainly mediocre results. The habit some commentators developed of calling him "Benjamin" rather than "Benson" shows that Lossing's fame had limits.[25]

Why have I expended so much effort on a forgotten, often forgettable historian? My broadest answer would be that few scholars have examined even Lossing's best works or those of similar contemporary writers. A study of Lossing thus offers insights into a vast range of historical writings that historians of history have, to date, ignored. We can view Lossing as one of many influential, if shallow, thinkers of nineteenth-century America, one of "scores of men [and women] who, in varying ways and with varying results, strove to bring intellectual order out of the chaos presented by the unrelated flow of experience."[26]

In 1886, one book reviewer alluded to such writers' importance, calling them "middle-men" who played a crucial role in making the public aware of the past.

In the historical field, as in every other, the function of the middle-man is just as essential as that of the original investigator. Indeed, if one were to measure the comparative importance of these two functions by the size of the constituency which the middle-man and the original investigator respectively address, the advantage might seem to be on the side of the middle-man.[27]

Even academicians, whose credentials encourage them to disparage Lossing and his ilk, have granted that such writers deserve study. "We should not ignore the popular historians," one commented, "if we wish to understand the growth of history. They show us in what manner popular taste has limited the performance of the historian . . . Such writers, historians or what not, are, intellectually speaking, nothing less than men of commerce."[28] We know little about these writers' impact on American readers, either in their time or later. This study cannot describe that impact definitively, but it can start to explicate its parameters. A biography of Lossing can thus serve as a prolegomenon to a richer but more elusive theme: the history of historical thought in American culture.

NOTES

1. "Literary and Intellectual Distinction," *Southern Literary Messenger* 6 (September 1840): 699. For similar ideas three decades later, see "Spurious History," *New York Observer* 11 January 1872, Secular Department, p. 1 col. 4-5. See also Francis Lieber to Unidentified [Frank Moore?], 21 November 1862, Lieber Correspondence, Library of Congress: "The distinction between 'a professional author' and a man of business does no longer exist in the same degree in which it was at least, believed, formerly, to exist."

2. William F. Poole, "A Popular Cyclopedia of United States History," *The Dial* [Chicago] 2 (January 1882): 209.

3. Moses Coit Tyler Diary, 4 February 1874, Cornell University Library, Ithaca, N.Y. Tyler recorded a comment of George H. Moore, Librarian, New-York Historical Society. A contemporary reference to Moore appeared in S. Austin Allibone, *A Critical Dictionary of English Literature and British and American Authors Living and Deceased*, Vol. 2 (Philadelphia: J. B. Lippincott & Co., 1882), 1352; see also Pamela Spence Richards, *Scholars and Gentlemen: The Library of the New-York Historical Society 1804-1982* (Hamden, Conn.: Archon Books, 1984), pp. 34-44.

4. Lossing, *The Pictorial Field-Book of the Revolution*, 30 parts (New York: Harper and Brothers, 1850-52); also in 2 Vols. (New York: Harper and Brothers, 1855, 1860); Lossing, *The Pictorial Field-Book of the War of 1812* (New York: Harper & Brothers, 1868).

5. Brantz Mayer to Lossing, 3 May 1869, Autograph File, Harvard University; W. C. Bryant to Lossing, 28 June 1873, LS 407, Lossing Addenda Box 16, Lossing Collection, Huntington Library, San Marino, California.

6. Peter G. Thomas to Draper, 26 October 1881, Draper Papers, Series DD, Vol. 15, p. 169, State Historical Society of Wisconsin; Lossing to Mrs. P. Edgewater [?], 31 January 1887, Lossing Collection, Perkins Library, Duke University.

7. For my purposes, an influential definition of culture appeared in Daniel Walker Howe, "American Victorianism as a Culture," *American Quarterly* 27 (December 1975): 509. Howe's essay, in turn, referred me to several more sources, including Clifford Geertz, "Ideology as a Cultural System," in Geertz, *The Interpretation of Cultures: Selected Essays* (New York: Basic Books, 1973), pp. [193]-233. See also Richard E. Sykes, "American Studies and the Concept of Culture: A Theory and Method," *American Quarterly* 15 (Summer 1963, Part Two): [253]-270, and the first chapter of Greg Urban, *A Discourse-Centered Approach to Culture: Native South American Myths and Rituals* in Texas Linguistics Series (Austin: University of Texas Press, 1991). Specifically on memory as a facet of culture, see, for example, David Thelen, "A New Approach to Understanding Human Memory Offers a Solution to the Crisis in the Study of History," *The Chronicle of Higher Education*, 27 September 1989, pp. B-1, B-3.

8. These understandings of culture bring us close to French scholars' concept of "mentalities"; for an assessable overview with a fine bibliography, see Jacques LeGoff, "Mentalities: A History of Ambiguities," in *Constructing the Past: Essays in Historical Methodology* ed. Jacques LeGoff and Pierre Nora (Cambridge]: Cambridge University Press; Paris: Editions De La Maison Des Sciences De L'Homme, 1985), pp. 166-80. Another good discussion was Michel Vovelle, *Ideologies and Mentalities*, trans. Eamon O'Flaherty (Chicago: The University of Chicago Press, 1990).

From a contrasting perspective, some historians question whether "culture" even signifies a meaningful concept, since (in their view) it focusses our attention too much on continuity and too little on change. See especially Karl J. Weintraub, *Visions of Culture* (Chicago & London: University of Chicago Press, 1966), p. 1n; and Immanuel Wallerstein, "What Can One Mean by Southern Culture?" in *The Evolution of Southern Culture*, ed. Numan V. Bartley (Athens and London: The University of Georgia Press, 1988), pp. 1-13. See also Michael A. Gismondi, "'The Gift of Theory': A Critique of the histoire des mentalites," *Social History* 10 (May 1985): 211-30.

9. Rev. George Diehl, "Practical Influence of Religious History," *The Evangelical Review* 9 (July 1857): 19-32; quotation from p. 20. Carl L. Becker, *Everyman His Own Historian: Essays on History and Politics* (New York: F. S. Crofts & Co., 1935), pp. [233]-55.

10. Efforts to define cultural history and (sometimes) distinguish it from intellectual history are legion. Some examples that stimulated my thinking include: Robert Darnton, "Intellectual and Cultural History," in *The Past Before Us: Contemporary Historical Writing in the United States*, ed. Michael Kammen (Ithaca, N.Y.: Cornell University Press for the American Historical Association, 1980), pp. 327-54; William J. Bouwsma, "Intellectual History in the 1980s: From History of Ideas to History of Meaning," *Journal of Interdisciplinary History* 12 (Autumn 1981): [279]-91; Roger Chartier, "Intellectual History and the History of *Mentalities*[:] A Dual Re-evaluation," in Chartier, *Cultural History: Between Practices and Representations*, trans. Lydia G. Cochrane (Cambridge: Polity Press, 1988), especially pp. 24-52; Robert Darnton, *The Great Cat Massacre and other Episodes in French Cultural History* (New York: Basic Books, Inc., 1984), pp. 257-63; Stefan Collini, "What is Intellectual History?" in *What is History Today?*, ed. Juliet Gardiner (Atlantic Highlands, N.J.: Humanities Press International, Inc., 1988), pp. 105-19; and two Donald R. Kelley essays: "Horizons of Intellectual History: Retrospect, Circumspect, Prospect," *Journal of the History of Ideas* 48 (January-March 1987): 143-69, and "What is Happening to the History of Ideas?" *Journal of the History of Ideas* 51 (January-March 1990): 3-25.

11. David Grimsted, "Introduction," in *Notions of the Americans, 1820-1860* (New York: George Braziller, 1970), p. 4. A more recent characterization of the field that has been significant for my thinking appeared in Lynn Hunt, "Introduction," *The New Cultural History* (Berkeley [et. al.]: University of California Press, 1989), p. 7.

12. Lewis O. Saum, *The Popular Mood in Pre-Civil War America* (Westport, Conn.: Greenwood Press, 1980), pp. 147-48.

13. Frederick Saunders and Thomas B. Thorpe, *Voice to America* (New York: Edward Walker, 1850), p. 300.

14. Undated manuscript in Charles Campbell Papers, Duke University.

15. Among many secondary sources on these researchers and writers, see especially George H. Callcott, *History in the United States, 1800-1860: Its Practice and Purpose* (Baltimore and London: The Johns Hopkins Press, 1970); David Lowenthal, *The Past*

Is a Foreign Country (Cambridge [et. al.]: Cambridge University Press, 1985), pp. 105-24.

16. William Nicholson, *American Edition of the British Encyclopedia*. 12 Vols. (Philadelphia: Mitchell, Ames, and White; Nashville: Ingram and Lloyd, 1819), IV, q.v. "History." This edition did not contain pagination.

17. See, for example, "History," *The Cabinet of Instruction, Literature and Amusement* [New York] 1 (6 June 1829): 650.

18. Some writings on popular culture that proved significant for my work included: Herbert J. Gans, *Popular Culture and High Culture: An Analysis and Evaluation of Taste* (New York: Basic Books, Inc., 1974); Carlo Ginzburg, *The Cheese and the Worms: The Cosmos of a Sixteenth-Century Miller*, trans. John and Anne Tedeschi (Baltimore and London: The Johns Hopkins University Press, 1980), pp. xiv-xxiv; Pierre Bourdieu, *Distinction: A Social Critique of the Judgement of Taste*, trans. Richard Nice (Cambridge, Mass.: Harvard University Press, 1984), pp. [1]-7; David Hall, "Introduction," in *Understanding Popular Culture: Europe from the Middle Ages to the Nineteenth Century*, ed. David Hall and Steven L. Kaplan (Berlin: Mouton Publishers, 1984), pp. [5]-18; Asa Briggs, "What is the History of Popular Culture?" in *What is History Today?*, pp. 120-30; Lawrence W. Levine, *Highbrow/Lowbrow: The Emergence of Cultural Hierarchy in America* (Cambridge, Mass.: Harvard University Press, 1988); David D. Hall, "Introduction," in *Worlds of Wonder, Days of Judgment: Popular Religious Belief in Early New England* (New York: Alfred A. Knopf, 1989), especially pp. 5-20; Tim Harris, "The Problem of 'Popular Political Culture' in Seventeenth Century London," *History of European Ideas* 10 (1) (1989): 43-58; Bob Scribner, "Is a History of Popular Culture Possible?" *History of European Ideas* 10 (2) (1989): 175-91; Kenneth Cmiel, *Democratic Eloquence: The Fight Over Popular Speech in Nineteenth-Century America* (New York: William Morrow and Co., 1990); *Rethinking Popular Culture: Contemporary Perspectives in Cultural Studies*, ed. Chandra Mukerji and Michael Schedson (Berkeley [et. al.]: University of California Press, 1991).

19. An influence on my ideas here was David Grimsted, "Books and Culture: Canned, Canonized, and Neglected," in *Needs and Opportunities in the History of the Book: America, 1639-1876*, ed. David D. Hall and John B. Hench (Worcester: American Antiquarian Society, 1987), pp. 187-225; see also Roger Chartier, "A Comment on Mr. Grimsted's Paper," pp. 226-32.

20. Even in our time, the relative ease with which individuals can enter the historical profession, according to some writers, renders professionalization models problematic for this field. See, for instance, Johan Huizinga, "The Task of Cultural History," in *Men and Ideas: History, the Middle Ages, the Renaissance: Essays*, trans. James S. Holmes and Hans Van Marie (New York: Meridian Books, 1959), p. 39.

21. Prescott to Unidentified, 25 November 1858 [?], Bancroft Library, University of California, Berkeley. For contemporary comments on Prescott, see Allibone, *Dictionary*, II: 1663-1675; "Prescott's Works," *Methodist Quarterly Review* 30 (January 1848): 1-28; "Prescott's Conquest of Peru," *Methodist Quarterly Review* (April 1848): 268-82. Among secondary sources, I especially benefitted from C. Harvey Gardiner, *Prescott and His Publishers* (Carbondale, Ill.: Southern Illinois University Press, 1959).

22. For instance, John Trumbull, *M'Fingal: An Epic Poem*, ed. Lossing (New York: J. P. Putnam, 1860 and later editions); Lossing, *A Biography of James A. Garfield* (Chicago: H. S. Goodspeed, 1882).

23. *Mathew Brady's Illustrated History of the Civil War*, (original edition New York: War Memorial Association, 1912); reprint edition (New York: The Fairfax Press, n.d.), p. 2.

24. H[erbert] Butterfield, *The Whig Interpretation of History* (New York: Charles Scribner's Sons, 1951). On this book, see John Clive, *Not By Fact Alone: Essays on the Writing and Reading of History* (New York: Alfred A. Knopf, 1989), pp. 286-96.

25. See, for instance, Horatio Potter envelope with his letter to Lossing, 18 November 1863, Lossing Collection, Rutherford B. Hayes Library, Fremont, Ohio, Box 7; Joel Munsell receipt to Lossing, 21 July 1871, *Ibid.*, Box 6; Thomas L. Cottin to Lossing, 12 October 1888, Lossing Papers, New York Public Library. See also Daniel Boorstin, *The Americans: The National Experience* (New York: Random House, 1965), p 382. One obituary avoided that error, but transposed Lossing's first and second given names: "John Benson Lossing Dead," *Detroit Free Press* 5 June 1891, p. 1 col. 6. An exhibition pamphlet referred to "J. Lossing Benson:" Joseph S. Van Why, *Hartford as a Publishing Center in the Nineteenth Century* (Hartford: Stowe Day Foundation, 1971), p. 3.

26. Bert James Loewenberg, *American History in American Thought: Christopher Columbus to Henry Adams* (New York: Simon and Schuster, 1972), p. 328.

27. "Books and Writers. Minor Historical Literature," *The Sunday School Times* 28 (10 April 1886): 234.

28. John Spencer Bassett, *The Middle Group of American Historians* (New York: The Macmillan Co., 1917), pp. 23, 136.

2

A SPARK FLAMED:
1813–1838

In an autobiographical sketch, Benson Lossing remarked that he was "a 'self-made' man[.]" After rising from an impoverished childhood, Lossing took pride in how work and moral earnestness won him a comfortable living and public acclaim. For himself and others, Lossing's career suggested that, in America, application of even modest gifts would bring rewards.[1] Like the stories of his contemporary Horatio Alger, Lossing's personal history seemed to prove the validity of the nation's ideals.

Lossing's perspective had some truth. At birth his socio-economic standing was low, even for rural Dutchess County, New York.[2] As a youth, Lossing lacked the extensive the formal education that might have made his progress easier. One scholar correctly noted that "Lossing had a spark"[3]—a spark of intellectual and commercial ambition that, once flamed, helped him attain solid literary success in his twenties and much more before he reached middle age.

But Lossing's climb to fame and fortune, though steady, was not uninterrupted. Early editorial work helped him develop favorite themes, but his periodicals never enjoyed commercial success. His first book gained him a foothold with a major New York publisher—Harper & Brothers—but this did not bear fruit for a decade. Even after Lossing won a reputation, his books' commercial fortunes proved variable, dependent on the economy and other historians' activities. Thus Lossing's self-characterization oversimplified how his career reflected the complexities of cultural development in nineteenth-century America.

Little information has survived about John (1768-1813), Benson Lossing's father. Like his Dutch ancestors, John farmed near Beekman, New York. His religious affiliations were fluid. Once Lossing described his father as "a pious Methodist[.]" But elsewhere Lossing wrote of both parents that "[t]hey were Friends or Quakers."[4]   A probable answer to this discrepancy is that both were Quakers in early life but later joined the Methodists.   In America's antebellum "Spiritual Hothouse," Methodism attracted members from various older sects; the Lossings offered an example.[5]   Sources regarding John's wife support this inference.

In January 1793, John married Miriam Dorland, the daughter of a blacksmith, who, like John, was of Dutch lineage. Miriam was a Quaker by birth who joined her husband in the Methodist Church.[6] Miriam and John had nine children, three of whom survived into adulthood: two daughters and their son Benson, born on February 12, 1813, at their home near Beekman. Lossing recalled that he owed his first name to Judge Egbert Benson, "one of the sturdy patriots of . . . my native county, during the stormy period of the Revolution and the formative one of our National Government . . . . My father was his friend and admirer, and testified his esteem by giving his son his name."[7]

A gazetteer from the year of Lossing's birth noted that Dutchess County "is one of the most opulent farming counties in the state." But the same writer commented that around Beekman the soil was thin "and much exausted [sic] in general." Still, the town had a population of almost 4,000, just 700 less than the county seat, Poughkeepsie. Over the next few decades, however, Poughkeepsie grew at the expense of Beekman and other communities. Lossing joined the rural youths who helped bring about this shift; but that happened only after several changes happened in his life.[8]

Some events from Lossing's childhood deserve comment because they accentuated his self-dependence. Just eight months after Lossing's birth, his father died "of billious cholic[.]"[9] Miriam then moved with her children to the farm of her brother, Samuel Dorland. Lossing got along well with his uncle's family and lived on that farm until his eleventh year, when calamity struck again: in August 1824, his mother died. The cause of her death never appeared in accounts of Lossing's life; he noted only that she "died an exemplary Christian[.]" But whatever spiritual consolation Lossing found later, at the time her passing only unsettled his life. After his mother died, Lossing stayed with a cousin near Washington Hollow "to learn the business of a farmer;"[10] but poor health forced him to abandon these efforts. Thus before his fourteenth birthday, Lossing perceived that he would have to carve his niche through other avenues. He felt compelled, as one biographer wrote, "to enter the field of toil, and battle for his daily bread."[11]

In October 1826, Lossing began to forge a path through that field by gaining an apprenticeship with Adam Henderson, a watchmaker and silversmith in Poughkeepsie. Lossing, like many local youths, thus cast his lot in the county's growing commercial center, a town that also held promise for cultural enterprise.[12] Lossing's apprenticeship of nearly seven years proved significant on several levels.   The training itself gave Lossing experience in careful, detailed work that later proved valuable for his engraving business. By age nineteen, he possessed sufficient dexterity to single-handedly make clocks.[13] Lossing did not need to progress far to become a competent engraver.

Other developments intimated Lossing's literary and historical interests. His biographers have noted how he read the few books he could find through these years. Some have contended that Lossing's challenge proved especially burdensome because Henderson's treatment was "severe." Not only did Henderson require him "to work very incessantly," but living conditions were rigorous. According to one pamphlet, the master would not allow Lossing to make a fire on Sundays, and many times the boy read in bed on the Sabbath, pulling blankets around himself to keep warm. But young Lossing persevered, rising early and remaining awake late to improve his mind through books.[14]

Most of Lossing's biographers agreed on books he read, although they did not identify sources for this information. Lossing's only comment was that he was "ever studious and eager for Knowledge[.]"[15] The Bible proved a foundational influence on Lossing, most importantly for his spiritual life. His religious beliefs at this time remain obscure, but later diaries suggest that as a young adult he was already an active and committed Christian. Perhaps the Scriptures also gave Lossing a model for historical and biographical writing, and heightened his sensitivity to a Providential interpretation of events. Such concepts later proved central to many of his writings.

Historical interest developed further when Lossing read a volume of John Marshall's *Life of George Washington*. One commentator found great significance in his perusal of this work, arguing that it marked "the beginning of a fascination with the first great American hero which would continue until Lossing's death."[16] But the volumes of Marshall's work varied in the attention they paid to Washington; in some, the Patriot barely intruded for hundreds of pages while Marshall traced military and political events. Since we do not know what part Lossing read, the *Life*'s impact remains unclear. But it probably helped to make Lossing aware of the American Revolution as a topic of study and of biographical writing as a means of approaching historical themes.

Lossing also read parts of Edward Gibbon's *Decline and Fall of the Roman Empire*. Gibbon, one writer thought, served as "the incentive and first inspiration"[17] for Lossing to enter a career of historical research and writing. As with Marshall's biography of Washington, no record survives that suggests the sections of Gibbon's vast work Lossing actually read. He might not have seen the eighteenth-century historian's attacks on Christianity; or, if he read them, Lossing could have chosen not to take them seriously.

Other influences of Gibbon perhaps took a more positive turn. For one, Gibbon's emphasis on the mutability of human institutions (especially the

Empire itself) might have appealed to a farm youth who could take comfort in the thought that powerful elites often fall into oblivion. Second, the *Decline*'s panoramic geographical and chronological perspective may have fed Lossing's ambition to study history on a worldwide or "universal" scale. This was the type of history Lossing first tried to write, before finding more success in concentrating on American themes. Finally, Gibbon's strong authorial presence might have taught Lossing that vital historical writing grows from personal involvement with places, people, and events. If this insight indeed came from Gibbon, that writer had a major influence on Lossing's career.[18]

Accounts of Lossing's youth have intimated that Henderson's regimen extended to forbidding him paper and writing instruments, but that the youth rose above this to write "acceptably" for local newspapers.[19] Lossing, then in his late teens, began such writing around 1830. Relatively little of this material survived; what did mostly consisted of mediocre poetry. An 1832 composition on "Christmas" in the *Poughkeepsie Telegraph* included an introductory paragraph in which the editor described the piece's author as "a young gentleman of this village, who is employed during the day in the acquirement of a mechanical art, and in leasure [sic] moments devotes his time to intellectual cultivation."[20]

Lossing turned twenty in 1833, and several important changes occurred. His apprenticeship ended early that year. In April, Henderson accepted Lossing as a full partner in his business, with the new firm taking the logical title of Henderson & Lossing. Advertisements for the partnership alerted readers that the Henderson-Lossing team was a "New Firm" offering "New Goods" to prospective customers.[21]

The business connection soon acquired familial overtones. On June 18, 1833, Lossing married Alice Barritt, who was Henderson's niece and the daughter of an English emigrant. Alice was around twenty when the couple took their vows at Christ Episcopal Church in Poughkeepsie.[22] Little evidence survives that sheds any light on their marriage. Alice and Lossing did not have any children together, although they adopted a daughter at an unknown date. When Alice died twenty years later, Lossing's effusive expressions of grief were sincere. Thus the relationship probably was happy for both parties.

During his partnership with Henderson, Lossing continued to write poetry. In January 1834, Lossing began a 64-line poem, entitled "Columbia," that summarized his style and ideas in this period. The second stanza analyzed reasons Lossing thought the United States might enter a Golden Age. "Whenever we look over the wide-spaced domain/ Joy, Peace and Tranquility pleases [sic] the eye/ Save the harmless contentions of party opinion/ Which stronger cements our political tie[.]"

Even the problems that had not yet disappeared in the U.S. were, for Lossing, on the wane. One example was the loosened hold of intemperance on the working classes. Although Lossing adhered to the Democratic Party in these years, he expressed thoughts more common to Whigs regarding the need to combat drunkenness. Rising above this evil, "[t]he Genius of Temp'rance its flag hath erected/ And never may that blessed Banner be furled/ 'Till its wise and benevolent scheme is effected/ The death of a gorgon—the reform of a world[.]"[23]

Lossing's evolving outlook on the wonders of American civilization also surfaced in prose compositions. In 1835 he wrote an Independence Day address that rang out changes through many conventional patriotic chords. There Lossing celebrated the possibilities of an ambitious individual rising above even a lowly social condition. "Here the Highroad to Honor and Distinction is broad, and it is trodden with equal success and applause by the man whose morning sky was clouded by poverty as by him whose early years were illuminated by the splendor of wealth and name." He specifically praised egalitarianism in gender roles, noting how oppression of women was evaporating in America. As a result of this liberation, Lossing cited women's contributions to national literature. Still, most American women's highest calling remained motherhood. "Her empire is an empire of love and under her tuition the child is taught those great moral principles which are to be his future passport to greatness, and it was to such early lessons from the life of piety that Washington ascribed his honors."[24]

This oration epitomized the optimism that remained prominent in Lossing's thinking throughout his life. In this speech, as in many other writings, Lossing did not exhibit striking originality. His comments about American women's opportunities and the nation's need to encourage their maternal instincts reflected middle-class concerns to solidify domesticity in an era when industrialism and urbanism threatened familial values.[25] Still, Lossing used this presentation to reveal his talent for cogent (albeit self-satisfied) social commentary. In the months after that speech, he learned to depend on such abilities for his livelihood.

Like much of Lossing's youth, the Henderson & Lossing partnership's history is obscure. We know that, in September 1835, the connection "dissolved" (Lossing's word) after twenty-seven months. Later commentators interpreted this event in two ways. Some argued that the firm's commercial fortunes had little to do with its demise; rather, Lossing ended the partnership because literary ambition compelled him to enter newspaper work. Others called the partnership "not only unsuccessful, but disastrous, pecuniarily," so that Lossing "relinquished it" to remain solvent. Lossing remembered the event vaguely; without offering specifics he called the partnership "unfortunate[.]"[26]

Circumstances must have seemed unfortunate for Lossing at that point; he was casting about for new means of making a living. When the connection with Henderson ended, he recalled, "I found myself much in debt, with no capital but my brain and muscles[.]" If Lossing doubted his resources, that did not render him inactive. In October 1835, a month after the earlier partnership collapsed, Lossing formed a connection "with Mr. [Egbert] Killey, in the publication of the *Poughkeepsie Telegraph*, the official (Democratic) paper of Dutchess County."[27]   As he had a decade before, Lossing quickly regrouped from a reversal and started constructing a new career, this time in writing and editorial work.

Lossing wrote in the *Telegraph* for five years before taking a direct role in the paper's fortunes. This involvement helped to convince Killey to make him a partner despite his straitened fiscal condition. The paper had gone through several changes in name and ownership since its 1824 origins. Its political leanings were toward the Democrats, but in complex ways because the New York Democrats were internally split into factions that, like the party's opponents, frequently shifted their ideological agendas.[28]

One commentator wrote that when Lossing joined the *Telegraph*, the paper sold 2,300 copies per issue. By 1839, this had risen to over 2,600, a figure it claimed "is larger, doubtless, than any country paper in the State."[29]   Even if we accept these statements as accurate, the paper's condition in the months after Lossing came aboard is difficult to assess. This is important because it obscures the young editors' motivations in starting another publication. On January 2, 1836, out of desperation or hope, Killey and Lossing began publishing a semi-monthly literary magazine, the *Poughkeepsie Casket*.

In choosing this title, Killey and Lossing were not indulging a taste for macabre humor. As a historical dictionary noted, nineteenth-century writers "[s]ometimes used [Casket] as the title of a selection of musical or literary 'gems.'"[30]

The magazine appeared through 1836, then Lossing and Killey suspended it during the financial panic of 1837. They re-started the *Casket* in April 1838, and it appeared regularly for three more years, before finally succumbing to chronic financial problems.

The *Casket* presented a forum for themes that, to varying degrees, concerned Lossing throughout his life. These included reform (especially in education, women's rights and, to a lesser extent, temperance), biography, and history.   It also suggested the type of historian Lossing hoped to become: a "philosophic" cultural scholar emphasizing classical and European studies. These plans later changed radically, and those changes reshaped Lossing's career.[31]

In the *Casket*'s first year, historical motifs surfaced occasionally, often in unconventional ways. An article on "Constantinople and its Associations" combined history and a travelogue in ways that later defined much of Lossing's career. Sometimes material on the Revolutionary War appeared, usually as memoirs or original accounts of events.[32]

The topic discussed most consistently in the early *Casket* was education. Some articles surmounted generalities about education's virtues and discussed specific academic fields. In one essay, Killey and Lossing discussed what they deemed to be a helpful approach to historical study. Ostensibly a meditation on "wholesome reading," this essay concentrated so much on historical literature that it expressed important aspects of the young editors' historiographical assumptions and program.[33]

First Lossing and Killey noted how reading lets us commune with humankind's "patriarchs," to "partake and imbibe" lessons from "the ancient fathers of Science, Philosophy and Religion, and in the mirror of imagination see reflected in pantomime, all which makes History interesting and useful." This act of "imagination" allows students to overcome their confining culture and understand the past on its own terms. Such careful study lends the rich reward of self-understanding as the reader "sits upon the apex of a great eminence, whence he beholds a panoramic view of the world, from the transactions in the Garden to the present moment."

Briefly overcoming their flowery language, the editors described the lessons of political history that made this a fertile field for reflective Americans. Like earlier commentators describing the rise, decline, and fall of states, and like Thomas Cole in his "Course of Empire" paintings, they offered a Machiavellian analysis of how societies, after luxury weakened them, lost a sense of virtue and fell prey to more austere nations. The history of Greece and Rome—each passing from republic to decadent, overextended empire, finally collapsing into smaller successor states—offered parallels from which Americans should recognize dangers to their political system.

For grasping such themes, readers needed some system for concentrating on important historical books, especially "[a]t the present day, when the prolific PRESS is overflowing with every production[.]" Hence "it is very important for the reader to use the utmost care in his selections; for unprofitable reading is time criminally thrown away." They suggested a plan by the French savant Nicolas Lenglet du Fresnoy, "who probably was as great a reader as ever took a book in hand[.]" He had developed an approach by which students could "acquire a universal knowledge of history" by reading six hours a day for ten and a half years! Lossing and Killey, with typical seriousness, concluded with an endorsement of this regimen.[34]

Despite their intellectual ambition, Killey and Lossing realized that their magazine was not a commercial success; so after a year's "experiment" with the *Casket*, they announced its expiration.[35] Despite a comment that they would include more literary writings in the *Telegraph*,[36] Killey and Lossing did not publish many such articles in early 1837. But this period ended with an event that held great significance for Lossing's career: in May 1837, he traveled to New York and began learning techniques of wood engraving from Joseph A. Adams.[37]

When Lossing contacted him, Adams was one of five wood engravers in New York. A New Jersey native, Adams came to the city around 1824, working for a time as a printer while experimenting with techniques for cutting images in wood. Adams received training from Alexander Anderson, then the preeminent engraver in America. By the early 1830s, his work began appearing in books and magazines, and soon Adams attained a very good reputation. A literary newspaper asserted that "[i]t is a matter of astonishment that we already have a few engravers on wood that cannot be exceeded anywhere; among the most conspicuous of whom is Mr. Adams[.]" Adams' most famous effort appeared in the illustrations he prepared for *Harper's Illuminated Bible* (1843).[38]

Adams taught Lossing for a few weeks and received $50 for the instruction. Biographical accounts agreed that Lossing proved an adept pupil because his background in watchmaking and silversmithing prepared him for detailed engraving work. Although brief, this episode was important for Lossing's career, not only for his new skills, but because the time with Adams made Lossing more aware of New York as a place of literary and artistic endeavor.[39]

By June 1837, Lossing returned to Poughkeepsie and threw himself into writing and editing projects. The immediate outlet for his efforts was the *Telegraph*, which suddenly began publishing more essays on educational, historical, and literary topics. Some of these featured Lossing's engravings, as he applied his new skills.[40]   Then, in April 1838, Killey and Lossing reinitiated the *Casket*.

The *Casket*'s second volume included a column that articulated the editors' goals and methods for realizing them. Seeking a wide readership, Killey and Lossing kept their magazine's interests broad. "It shall be our aim," they remarked, "to present to the reading community subjects suited to the capacities and tastes of every virtuous class—the child as well as the adult—keeping constantly in view those great cardinal principles of morality which elevate the standard of moral excellence, and enrich the understanding."[41] They also noted Lossing's engravings as a new feature.

Lossing's interest in artistic endeavors led him to compose several "Letters" on drawing. Addressing himself to "Young Ladies," as the audience most devoted to this "pleasing amusement" and "beautiful branch of fashionable accomplishment," he stressed drawing's utility for a traveler who, by sketching scenes she has visited, can "bring to mind the recollection of circumstances which have escaped the memory in the lapse of years[.]"[42] Ten years later, researching his most famous book, Lossing made this advice central to his historical method.

The new *Casket* contained several essays on historiography. Lossing did not write many of these, but their inclusion was significant for his developing perspective on historical theory and practice. One article emphasized a command of chronology and geography as useful for historical investigators; comments on the latter discipline presaged the approach Lossing took in his *Field Books*: "a knowledge of the places where illustrious events have occurred . . . by affording a nucleus around which the mind can gather its acquisitions, and a definite spot where to locate scenes and events, impresses their history upon the mind with a definiteness and reality that no other means could acquire."[43]

The magazine contained occasional references to contemporary historians. Like Lossing's topical writings, these intimated interests he developed over later years. Especially prominent were references to William Dunlap, a conservative New York artist, dramatist, and historian. A suggestion of a benefit for Dunlap drew an enthusiastic response in the *Casket*. "[C]itizens of New-York cannot extend their benevolence to a more worthy cause, or a more meritorious man."[44]

References to Dunlap affirmed two important themes in Lossing's professional life. First, knowing someone who was at once a historian and a practitioner of a fine art encouraged Lossing to hope he could imitate the combination of those specialties. Second, Dunlap, like many other literary and artistic figures Lossing came to admire, forged his career in New York, which by the 1830s stood as the nation's commercial and intellectual center. The examples of Dunlap and others encouraged Lossing to view New York as a favorable place to base his career. His time with Joseph Adams also helped make Lossing aware of the metropolis' resources, and just over a year later he decided to leave Poughkeepsie in favor of the more competitive arena.[45]

This decision required encouragement. That came when publishers of *The Family Magazine*, a general interest weekly in the city, approached him about assuming editorial duties with their paper. In late 1838 he accepted, hoping to juggle the new responsibilities with work in Poughkeepsie.[46] He also wanted to start an engraving firm in New York. Once there, Lossing advanced on all these fronts; but he did so only after his first book—an *Outline History of the Fine Arts*—proved a failure and caused Lossing to reevaluate his career.

NOTES

1. Benson J. Lossing autobiography manuscript, LS 1055, Lossing Addenda Box 23, Lossing Papers, Henry B. Huntington Library, San Marino, California. This manuscript was apparently the source for the Lossing entry in *The National Cyclopaedia of American Biography* (New York: James T. White & Co., 1893), IV: 324. Several contemporary sources employed this phrase to describe Lossing. An undated, unidentifiable newspaper column in the Lossing Papers, Box 17, Rutherford B. Hayes Library, Fremont, Ohio, characterized Lossing as one of "[t]he Self-made Men of our Times." An engraving of Lossing in the Lee Kohns Memorial Collection, New York Public Library, used the same phrase as a caption.

2. Controversy has persisted over whether to include the "t" in "Dutchess"; in the 1880s Lossing engaged in some of these discussions. Although Lossing and others wanted to drop that letter, I have retained the more common spelling. See Anne W. Young, "Dutchess Or Duchess," *The Dutchess* 1 (September 1973): 2-4.

3. Alexander Davidson, Jr., "How Benson J. Lossing Wrote His 'Field Books' of the Revolution, the War of 1812 and the Civil War," *The Papers of The Bibliographical Society of America* 32 (1938): 57.

4. Lossing journal, LS 1116, Lossing Collection, Huntington Library; Autobiography, LS 1055, Lossing Addenda Box 23, same collection.

5. Jon Butler, *Awash in a Sea of Faith: Christianizing the American People* (Cambridge, Mass. and London: Harvard University Press, 1990), pp. 236-41.

6. *American Ancestry III*: 182; files of the *Poughkeepsie Journal*.

7. Benson J. Lossing to Henry F. Drowne 12 October 1867, Drowne Papers, Brown University Library. On Benson, see Charles W. Spencer's article in *Dictionary of American Biography*, ed. Allen Johnson (New York: Charles Scribner's Sons, 1929), II: 204. The *Poughkeepsie Journal* for early 1813 made no mention of Lossing's birth, which was not surprising given its concern over the war with England.

8. Horatio Gates Spafford, *A Gazetteer of the State of New-York* (Albany: H. C. Southwick, 1813), pp. 73, 74, 131; Barbara Shupe, Janet Steins, and Jyoti Pandit, *New York State Population: 1790-1980* (New York, London: Neal-Schuman Publishers, Inc., 1987), pp. 20, 242.

9. Lossing 1853 journal, LS 1116, Lossing Collection, Huntington Library. I could not find a reference to John's death in the *Poughkeepsie Journal*, although several issues of that weekly newspaper were missing from the microfilm which I read. A reference to John Lossing's will appeared in "Dutchess County Wills, Book D," *The Dutchess* 9 (Spring 1982): 28.

10. Both quotations from 1853 journal, LS 1116, Lossing Collection, Huntington Library.

11. Biographical sketch in *Commemorative Biographical Record of the Counties of Dutchess and Putnam, New York* (Chicago: J. H. Beers & Co., 1897), Part 2, p. 1058.

12. On Lossing's apprenticeship with Henderson, see George Barton Cutten and Amy Pearce Ver Nooy, "The Silversmiths of Poughkeepsie," *Dutchess County Historical Society Year Book* 30 (1945): 23-41, especially pp. 32-35. On nineteenth-century social mobility in Poughkeepsie, see Clyde and Sally Griffen, *Natives and Newcomers: The Ordering of Opportunity in Mid-Nineteenth-Century Poughkeepsie* (Cambridge, Mass. and London: Harvard University Press, 1978).

13. Nathaniel Paine, *A Biographical Notice of Benson John Lossing, LL.D.* (Worcester, Mass.: Privately Printed, 1892), p. 4.

14. Ibid.

15. 1884 autobiography, LS 1055, Lossing Addenda Box 23, Lossing Collection, Huntington Library.

16. J. Tracy Power, "Benson J. Lossing," in *American Historians, 1607-1865*, ed. Clyde N. Wilson, Vol. 30 of *Dictionary of Literary Biography* (Detroit: Gale Research Company, 1984), p. 164.

17. Paine, *Biographical Notice*.

18. Excellent secondary sources on Gibbon are numerous; see especially Patricia B. Craddock, *Edward Gibbon, Luminous Historian, 1772-1794* (Baltimore and London: Johns Hopkins University Press, 1989).

19. Paine, *Biographical Notice*; Mary L.D. Ferris, "Benson J. Lossing, LL.D.," *American Author* 1 (May 1902): 101-5. Lossing's 1884 autobiography did not mention this supposed harsh treatment.

20. "Christmas," typescript from *Poughkeepsie Telegraph* 19 December 1832, Vassar College Archives, Vassar College Library, Poughkeepsie, New York.

21. Henderson-Lossing advertisement, *Poughkeepsie Telegraph* 26 June 1833 p. 4 col. 5; W[illiam]. S. Baker, *Medallic Portraits of Washington* (Philadelphia: Robert M. Lindsay, 1885), p. 209, had a description of the firm's business cards.

22. *The Records of Christ Church Poughkeepsie New York* 2 Vols. ([Poughkeepsie: Christ Church]: 1916), II: 211, in a misprint, gave the parties to the 18 June 1833 wedding as Else Barritt and Benson J. Lawson.

23. Both poems in Lossing Album, American Antiquarian Society.

24. Lossing Address in Hopewell Church, 4 July 1835, LS 1047, Lossing Addenda Box 1, Lossing Papers, Huntington Library, pp. 14, 15.

25. On style and content in such speeches, see Henry A. Hawken, *Trumpets of Glory: Fourth of July Orations, 1786-1861* (Granby, Conn.: The Salmon Brook Historical Society, 1976). On women, see Nancy F. Cott, *The Bonds of Womanhood: "Woman's Sphere" in New England, 1780-1835* (New Haven and London: Yale University Press, 1977), and Linda K. Kerber, *Women of the Republic: Intellect and Ideology in Revolutionary America* (New York: Norton, 1980).

26. Paine, *Biographical Notice*; Ferris, "Benson J. Lossing"; undated "Self-made Men" clipping cited in note 1 above. "Benson John Lossing," *Appletons' Journal* 8 (20 July 1872): 68, used almost the same words. For the quote, see 1853 Lossing journal, LS 1116, Lossing Collection, Huntington Library.

27. 1853 Lossing journal, LS 1116, Lossing Collection, Huntington Library.

28. On the *Telegraph*'s history, see J. H. French, *Gazetteer of the State of New York* (n.p., 1861), p. 268n; and *The History of Dutchess County New York*, ed. Frank Hasbrouck (Poughkeepsie, N.Y.: S. A. Matthieu, 1909), pp. 242-44.

29. Amy Pearce Ver Nooy, "Dutchess County Men—Benson John Lossing," *Dutchess County Historical Society Yearbook* 30 (1945): 33.

30. *The Oxford English Dictionary*, ed. James A. H. Murray (Oxford Clarenton Press, 1933; reprinted 1961), II: 150. All of the *OED*'s examples of this usage were from 1850-1877. On the Hudson, N.Y. paper, see Neal L. Edgar, *A History and Bibliography of American Magazines 1810-1820* (Metuchen, N.J.: The Scarecrow Press, Inc., 1975), p. 117. At least one gift-book used the title: *The Casket: A Christmas and New Year's Present for Children and Young Persons* (Boston: Bowles and Dearborn, 1828).

31. One biographer (Paine, *Biographical Notice*, p. 4) credited him with writing "nearly all" of the magazine's contents. Since most *Casket* articles were unsigned, I cannot either verify or falsify this assertion. I have emphasized materials that Lossing either clearly wrote or in which he had an editorial hand. I mention some things he apparently did not write on the inference that he at least had some influence on their inclusion and so such material reflected his interests.

32. "Constantinople and its Associations," *Casket* 1 (13 February 1836): 29. This article was signed "L.J.B.," perhaps a conscious transposition of Lossing's initials to avoid the appearance that one person was writing most of the paper. See also "History. Battle of the Brandywine," *Casket* 1 (2 July 1836): 108-9; "Selections. Revolutionary History," *Casket* 1 (22 October 1836): 172.

33. See "A Dialogue on History," *Youth's Companion* [Boston] 5 (30 November 1831): 111-12; "The Philosophy of History," *American Magazine of Useful and Entertaining Knowledge* [Boston] 3 (October 1836): 14-15; Philomathes, "The Uses of Biography," *The Gentleman's Magazine* [Philadelphia] 2 (February 1838): [73]-77; Rev. Maurice W. Dwight [of Brooklyn], "The Guilt and Danger of Reading Infidel, Fictitious and Impure Works," *The American National Preacher* 12 (December 1838): 187.

34. "Reading," *Casket* 1 (7 May 1836): 79.   On Lenglet Du Fresnoy, see *Dictionnaire des Lettres Francaises* (Paris: Librairie Artheme Fayard, 1960), Vol. 3, Part 2, pp. 86-87. During the eighteenth century some of his books came into English translation. Most significant for the *Casket* essay was *New Method of Studying History* trans. Richard Rawlinson, 2 Vols. (London: Printed for W. Burton, 1728).   Among other discussions of historical reading, see "The Philosophy of History," *North American Review* 39 (July 1834): 30-56, especially pp. 52, 56; "Thoughts on the Manner of Writing History. Translated from the French," *Southern Literary Messenger* 3 (February 1837): 156-57; "W.S.", "On the Uses and Sources of History," *The Western Academician and Journal of Education and Science* [Cincinnati] 1 (May 1837): 128-40; "Reading of History," *The Princeton Review* 19 (April 1847): 211-23.   One English scholar cited the same reading program as Lossing and Killey, but found it too taxing. William Smyth, *Lectures on Modern History* (Boston: Benjamin B. Mussey and Co., 1849), p. 5.

35. "To Our Patrons," *Casket* 1 (3 December 1836): 199.

36. "Adieu," *Casket* 1 (17 December 1836): 203.

37. 1853 journal, LS 1116, Lossing Collection, Huntington Library.

38. The first quotation was from Sinclair Hamilton, "Early American Book Illustration," Appendix I in *American Literary Publishing Houses, 1638-1899 Part 2: N-Z,* ed. Peter Dzwonkoski, Vol. 49 of *Dictionary of Literary Biography* (Detroit: Gale Research Company, 1986), p. 511.   Another secondary source was Ralph C. Smith's article on Adams in *Dictionary of American Biography*, ed. Allen Johnson (New York: Charles Scribner's Sons, 1928), I: 93. The contemporary comment appeared in "Wood Engraving," *The New-York Mirror* 17 (18 April 1840): 343.

39. Paine, *Biographical Notice*.

40. See "Fountain of the Prince of Palestine," *Telegraph,* 28 June 1837 p. 1 col. 4-7 (this item was signed "L."); "Queen Victoria," *Telegraph*, 2 August 1837, p. 2 col. #1-2; "The Old Dutch House in Poughkeepsie," *Telegraph*, 6 September 1837, p. 1 col. 2.

41. "Salutatory," *Casket* 2 (21 April 1838): 7.

42. "The Artist. Drawing. Letter I.," *Casket* 2 (5 May 1838): 12. The "Drawing" series included eight "Letters," which appeared in issues dated 5 May to 8 September 1838.

43. Quotations from "Caius," "The Essayist. No. III.," *Casket* 2 (2 June 1838): 28-29. Other contributions to this series from the same writer that involved reflections on history included "No. II.," *Casket* 2 (19 May 1838): 20-21, and "No. IV.," *Casket* 2 (16 June 1838): 36-37.

44. "William Dunlap, Esq.," *Casket* 2 (3 November 1838): 119. See also David Grimsted, "William Dunlap," in *American Historians, 1607-1865,* ed. Clyde N. Wilson, pp. 77-84; Fred Moramorco, "The Early Drama Criticism of William Dunlap," *American Literature* 40 (March 1968): 9-14; Joseph J. Ellis, *After the Revolution: Profiles of Early American Culture* (New York: Norton, 1979).

45. It may have been significant that by the summer of 1837 Lossing's engravings appeared in New York periodicals; see clipping from the *Mirror*, 26 August 1837, in Lossing Collection, Vassar College, Box 8.

46. Lossing 1854 journal, LS 1116, Lossing Collection, Huntington Library.

3

HISTORIAN ON THE MAKE: 1838–1841

Moving to New York represented a crucial turn in Lossing's career. He remained in the city for thirty years before moving back to Dutchess County; thus New York served as his base while he produced some important books. But Lossing's first years in the metropolis left him with few achievements. During this time, he struggled as a "historian on the make" to survive a business depression and negative responses to his first book.

Lossing already had an awareness of how economic, technological, and other changes were transforming the American publishing industry; in moving to New York he placed himself at the focal point for these trends. Mechanical innovation—especially more efficient printing equipment, new type-casting techniques, and paper-making machinery—flooded America with books and periodicals in far greater numbers than was previously feasible. Distribution also changed, as itinerant book agents, such as Mason Weems, grew less common. The practice of soliciting subscribers for books before publication (the "subscription trade") went into decline, although it had a strong resurgence after the Civil War. For the first two decades of Lossing's career as a writer and illustrator, bookstores served as the major outlets for literary wares.

The "print revolution" fueled complex changes in publishers' and writers' marketing aims and strategies; two of them proved most important.[1] First, due to larger markets and more competition, publishers felt compelled to measure more intelligently the topics, approaches, or writers that appealed to the widest audience.[2] One English historian recognized the American market as crucial to any work's failure or success. "The reading community in the United States forms so large & important a proportion of those who speak our common language, that every English author must be deeply interested to know how his work is received among them[.]"[3] The same interest animated indigenous writers.

A second change involved publishers' new ability to print books in greater numbers and to do so more economically. Fierce competition encouraged them to produce as many books as possible from well-known writers or on what they perceived as popular topics, while using less durable binding and paper in hopes that low prices would attract readers. Some observers felt amazement that such an overwhelming flood of publications was available; many more attacked the "cheap books" phenomenon as so materialistic that it would ultimately damage the national spirit.[4]

Through his first years in New York, Lossing maintained a heavy load of editorial duties. He remained active with the *Poughkeepsie Telegraph*, although often his contributions were reprints from the *Casket* or *Family Magazine*.[5] Lossing's role in the *Casket* was more substantive, especially because he served as its only editor despite his distance from Poughkeepsie. Change and continuity in that magazine's contents reflected Lossing's efforts as he tried to carve out a niche in national letters.

In April 1839, Lossing, then the *Casket*'s only editor, began its third volume. In it, historical theory and practice, a theme in some earlier issues, grew more prominent. Lossing's desire to elucidate the nature and utility of historical knowledge remained evident. The most important new departures involved biography as an adjunct to history and Lossing's effort to write a history of civilization through studies in the fine arts.

Biographical essays appeared in the *Casket*'s early volumes,[6] but became far more frequent after Lossing's 1938 move to New York. One of the new series' first installments analyzed Sir Walter Raleigh, describing Raleigh as "a truly good and great man, and one of the brightest ornaments of the British throne during the reign of the 'Virgin Queen.'"[7] Yet the virtuous courier lost his life due to an ungrateful monarch's merest whim. This suggested that no human accomplishment offered real security; an individual's or nation's fortune could shift at any moment, and any placing of trust in temporal values was foolish.

Emphasis on mutability persisted in biographical articles; but it coexisted with other themes. As the biographical series gained momentum, Lossing used it to develop a "great-man" theory of history that found events' causes in particular individuals' fortitude, insight, or, in negative terms, their failures. For Lossing, such a belief in free will did not negate the significance of Providence or similar unseen forces in destiny's turns. An essay on the Indian religious thinker Rammohun Roy stressed the integrity that drove Roy to embrace Christianity and briefly serve as a means for his people's enlightenment. Yet individual genius and promise sometimes proved powerless before inexplicable decrees of fate or Deity. Roy, for example, died just as his career began.[8] The lesson was clear: apart from God's grace, no human being, however gifted, could avoid sudden, drastic shifts in fortune.

Sometimes Lossing analyzed American developments as variations on European themes. His clearest allusion to American values came as he criticized another writer's defense of Oliver Cromwell and praise of him as "a patriot" concerned "to rescue his enthralled countrymen, whose lives and comfort were the sport of a puerile prince." In a long editorial, Lossing dissented sharply from that argument. Ambition drove Cromwell, he contended, and "not that honest ambition that moves the heart and arm for country's sake, but ambition for personal greatness[.]" Lossing depicted Cromwell as standing in contrast to Washington. "And did he [Cromwell], when his work was accomplished, like a true patriot, like a virtuous Cincinatus, return to the plough? No: he eagerly grasped the proffered sceptre, and to show how conscious he was of the unholy means he had employed to obtain it, the four years of his power were years of misery[.]" Lossing explicitly contrasted Cromwell with the American Revolution's heroes, whose motives were so much purer. "Not so with . . . Washington and LaFayette. See how the former rebuked the colonel who dared to offer him a sceptre and a crown . . . . To this school of patriots Cromwell did not belong."[9]

Biographical studies soon merged with a new theme: the fine arts and their history. Lossing's interest in art history had appeared occasionally in the earlier *Casket*,[10] but it grew more prominent from 1839 into 1840, as Lossing prepared his book on the subject. Through the next year, several issues presented sections from the *Outline History* as lead articles.[11] But before that time, in April 1840, concern over the *Casket*'s financial problems and the press of other duties convinced Lossing that he should turn its editorial functions over to someone else. A connection that for several years represented Lossing's main outlet for writing and engraving ended, but he had no time to reflect on the event's significance, because he had so many other projects in motion.

After he severed ties to the *Casket*, Lossing devoted more energy to editing *The Family Magazine*, one of many "general knowledge" magazines of the era.[12] The weekly *Magazine* first appeared in April 1833. Its various editors (including Lossing for the last two volumes) kept it active for eight years. Afterward Lossing and others referred to *The Family Magazine* as "the first illustrated magazine published in this country."[13] Whatever validity this assertion possessed, *The Family Magazine*, even before Lossing's involvement, meshed well with his approach to learning.

In the *Magazine*'s sixth (1838-39) volume Lossing started to have an impact on it. This is demonstrated by the *Magazine*'s attention to Dutchess County and the use of engravings by Lossing's mentor, Joseph Adams.[14]

These changes were modest, both because other duties occupied Lossing's energy and because the *Magazine* was already to his liking. But soon Lossing stood poised to fashion the journal more as he wished.

The significance of historical theory and practice in Lossing's thinking grew evident in a preface to Volume Seven, where he remarked that the *Magazine*'s sources would encompass "the sunny fields of literature," especially "the sepulchre of the past whence History borrows her lore[.]"[15] His first issue's lead article, a biographical essay on Columbus, began fulfilling this promise with speculations on history's lessons. Lossing started with gloomy musings over the mutability of even the best institutions. "All history is but one vast record of alternate peace and discord—of reciprocal carnage and desolation among neighboring nations—of revolution and perpetual change . . . . Kingdoms and republics change geographical positions; each rise, flourish, and decay. And such is history."

But Lossing found cause for hope as he posited a "great-man theory" involving individuals who, "rising above the corrupt mass," offer "true images of deity. They are like the green oasis in the midst of the desert, and form a pleasing resting-place for the weary historian . . . . Of these was Christopher Columbus, the discoverer of this western world." This reiterated Lossing's emphasis on biography as an avenue to historical study.[16]

Volume Seven's most significant historical contributions came in Lossing's essays on the "Romance of History." These mostly traced events in European history, with medieval, French, and English topics predominant. The first paper, on the French Revolution, included reflections on why liberty and anarchy were directly contrary tendencies. True freedom and enlightenment sprang from Christian teachings; the impious forces that fueled France's Terror, on the other hand, represented "a most despotic and bloody power . . . . Anarchy in its most horrid form swayed the sceptre, and enlightened France, in the short space of a year, made a retrograde movement of at least four centuries."[17]

Another essay, although mentioning neither France or the United States, extracted from these nations' contrasted revolutions generalizations about historical tumults and their causes. Lossing emphasized citizens' "confidence or distrust in leaders" as a crucial variable. With the French experience in his thoughts, he remarked that "[w]hen suspicion of the integrity of rulers lights the fires of rebellion, and fans the flame of civil discord, then it is that the ambitious demagogue erects the throne of the despot amid the ruins of republicanism." But fortunately another model was available, as American history revealed. "On the other hand, where men are true to themselves and their country, a few may present an invulnerable phalanx, that can crush the powers of wrong and maintain for government, by such fidelity to principles, the exalted character of Equity and Equality."[18]   Already, even as he focussed on European topics, Lossing was developing ideas about how America had avoided errors of past societies.

Lossing's interest in art history climaxed in 1840 when Harper & Brothers gave him a contact to write an *Outline History of the Fine Arts*. This book was not critically successful, although it did appear in several editions.[19] But its failure was important for redirecting Lossing's career from stressing broad cultural development and theories about art to a focus on American history and practical applications for artistic craftsmanship.

In 1817, John and James Harper started a New York printing establishment, J. and J. Harper, launching their careers as publishers. In the mid-1820s, two younger brothers, Joseph Wesley and Fletcher, joined the company as partners; within another decade Harper & Brothers (the firm's official name from 1833) was the country's largest publisher. It published in a wide variety of genres, with important projects in philosophy, history, and fiction.[20]

By the 1830s, a depression in the book trade compelled the brothers to consider changes in their publishing concentrations. James wanted to specialize in non-fiction books, taking a cue from general knowledge magazines. As a result, Harpers started printing such works in series or "libraries" to which readers could subscribe. Their most important series included a School District Library and the Family Library.[21]

In the decade before Lossing's *Outline History*, the Family Library included several biographical and historical works, mostly on classical or Biblical topics. Reviews usually praised the series, although one journal criticized it on nationalistic grounds; too many of its writers were English. "[I]t is to be regretted that the Library is not more American in its character." Another magazine labeled some of the series' engravings "coarsely done[.]"[22] We do not know whether such criticism changed the firm's approach to the series. In giving the art history project to Lossing, they were exploiting indigenous talent, and he must have seemed a competent illustrator for the volume.

One writer suggested that Lossing first became familiar with the brothers through Joseph Adams, his engraving mentor. Whatever the specific sequence of events, around 1839 or 1840 Lossing began visiting the publisher's offices on Cliff Street. "Many of the most eminent authors and literary men had become associated with the House, and their reminiscences of Mr. [James] Harper's sage counsel and quaint humor would fill a volume," Lossing recalled of these visits. "But especially the young and as yet unknown author had occasion to remember the appreciation and encouragement received in the counting-room when he first met the oldest of the Harper brothers."[23]

James Harper admired Lossing's efforts in *The Family Magazine*. Aware that Lossing was not only a practicing engraver but also interested in past artists, Harper thought Lossing could write an illustrated art history survey for the Family Library series. Although the project was ambitious, Lossing was able to compose the text quickly. In the spring of 1840, Harpers published the *Outline History* as a volume in the Family Library; later it also appeared in the School District series. Based upon other writers' fees from this period, the publishers probably paid Lossing around $200 for the text and possibly more for the book's engravings.[24]

Lossing's handicaps in writing his first book were serious and ultimately fatal. Despite his earnestness and hard work, Lossing did not possess sufficient learning to distinguish important information in art history from extraneous material. This defect rendered the *Outline History* at once pedantic and superficial. Further, apart from William Dunlap's work on the arts in America, Lossing had few indigenous models available. Most existing volumes dealt with the field only in an anecdotal, noncritical way.[25]

Lossing used his introduction to state the *Outline History*'s goals. He explained that he wanted to create a short survey of art history "in a perspicuous manner and a cheap form[.]" He claimed to consider this necessary for American youths' moral elevation. In the arts, as in so many spheres, America was in a position to benefit from all history. Soon Lossing returned to this theme, depicting the United States as the last, best fruit of history (pp. [iii], iv). Reflecting such nationalistic ideas, Lossing devoted considerable attention to American art. Here he broached topics that interested many contemporary observers. Lossing's views on American art were neither profound nor particularly consistent, but they revealed his developing perspective on national culture.

Through the first half of the nineteenth century, the character and purposes of artistic enterprise in the United States were frequent concerns for both foreign and indigenous commentators.[26] In 1824, a British critic remarked that "[t]he FINE ARTS, generally, are neglected by the Americans."[27] Few writers in the United States doubted this assertion, but they argued vociferously over whether this represented a mark of shame or of pride. This overlapped with discussions of how to combat this artistic inferiority. Many, including William Dunlap, contended that more and better art would spring spontaneously from individuals' natural genius as economic development progressed.[28] Others contended that, for good or ill, Americans could never excel in artistic endeavors because a nonaristocratic society had no inclination to patronize artists. Others rejected this line of argument, suggesting instead that "[t]he true difficulty in the way of our artistic advancement is the want of taste in our people," a problem one writer labeled "the rage for cheapness."[29]

As if these issues were not complicated enough, the debate grew more involved as Americans tried to elucidate indigenous art's proper relationship to European culture. In the 1850s, with the rise of strong nativistic tendencies, this was an especially pressing topic, but it was present even before the *Outline History*. One writer stridently contended that American artists should imitate nature, not the European masters. The same observer thought that, because the United States possessed no subjects worthy of grand historical painting, its artists should concentrate on depicting the nation's landscapes.[30]

In a derivative fashion, Lossing found himself drawn in several directions as he considered these questions. Sometimes he worried that Americans tended to judge everything—including art—too much in terms of utility, spurning objects or ideas that lacked direct applicability to life. This was one reason American architecture had not yet achieved a "refined" state. "In our republic, architecture, like other departments of the fine arts, has yielded to the influences of a utile nature, which ever exists in a young and vigorous state" (pp. 92-93).

On one hand, Lossing criticized Americans for not having refined tastes like Europeans. But in practically the same breath, he worried over Americans' need to be culturally independent of Europe. Although he did not note this tension, Lossing probably meant that American "refinement," when it developed, would possess original qualities that owed nothing to the Old World.

Similar themes surfaced as Lossing deplored Americans' slim accomplishments in sculpture. His main point, as with architecture, was that "[t]he tastes and pursuits of the people of this country are of a strictly utilitarian character[.]" Rampant pragmatism already presented a threat to individual and collective virtue. "Our youthfulness warns us to build up bulwarks of every kind around this young Republic—our distance from works of European art prevents the general diffusion of a taste for such acquirements, and the avenues to wealth being so numerous, we are justly known by the cognomen, admitting of a national application, of money-getters."

Still, hope remained because American artists were gradually recognizing their history's richness as a source for art. "Our country is rich in historical incidents, worthy to be portrayed by the pencil, the chisel, or the pen of inspiration . . . . We have no mythological divinities, or supernatural exploits to exhibit in sculptured groups, but we have other scenes far more striking and grand, which shall yet call forth the mightiest efforts of genius, and add a new and brilliant gem to the diadem of American Renown" pp. 173, 174). The best means of attaining cultural maturity, Lossing argued, was for Americans to appreciate their history, to recall inspiring stories of the past and teach these to their children. Within a few years, Lossing came to see the realization of these aims as his life's work.

Lossing's scholarly limitations did not escape the notice of reviewers who discussed the *Outline History*. A relatively innocuous column appeared in *The New-York Mirror*, a literary and artistic newspaper. After implicitly praising Lossing for attempting a difficult but necessary task, the *Mirror* commented that his book would likely prove of little use to either scholars or general readers. "As it contains nothing to make it particularly valuable to men of taste or knowledge in art, we presume it was meant for general readers; and if so, the explanations of technical language should have been much fuller." The *Mirror*'s columnist briefly touched on "the general carelessness of the volume," then restated the conviction that Lossing's book filled no meaningful need. "The 'Outline History' will answer very well, when there is no better authority to be had, and only then."[31]

The unkindest cuts of all came from *The New York Review*, an articulate literary journal that enjoyed a high reputation at the time. Its notice savaged the *Outline History*, observing that "such a history as we have here can rightfully claim a place in no library. It wants the first requisite of a historical work, accuracy in the statement of facts; it is a crude compilation, carelessly put together, without order, and without examination of the authorities upon which it relies." The reviewer thought the book should have dispensed with "all the frivolous anecdotes, to make room for something better in the modern part of the history, than the pitifully meagre account it now presents. Not the slightest notion can be gathered from it what architecture, or sculpture, or painting, has been since the revival of these arts[.]"

Passing from the treatment of architecture to other arts, the review turned sarcastic. "And so in sculpture, there are but few names upon whom he deigns to confer the immortality of a record in his imperishable volume, which however is not half so bad as the wretched manner in which he has murdered the fame of those he has undertaken to honor[.]" Finally the irked reviewer gave up trying to list all the book's problems: "[I]t would be a hopeless task to attempt to point out [all] the defects of this volume; it is in no sense of the word a history of the Arts, and is throughout imperfect, inaccurate, and confused; it abounds in typographical errors, and its wood cut illustrations are in perfect keeping with the rest."[32]

With reviews like these, the *Outline History* inevitably hindered Lossing's literary career. We do not know how deeply the book's failure hurt Lossing, since no relevant manuscripts have survived from this period. But he did stop writing for publication for about five years. Apparently the negative experience with his first volume dissuaded Lossing from thinking he could succeed as an historian. Instead, he focussed his attention on his engraving business. Lossing still harbored ambitions to write, since at the end of that time he jumped at new offers to produce books and edit magazines. When that happened, Lossing's cloudy literary horizon started to reveal glimmers of sunlight.

NOTES

1. A discussion of these changes appeared in Carl Bode, *The Anatomy of American Popular Culture 1840-1861* (Berkeley and Los Angeles: University of California Press, 1959), pp. 109-11. See also Rollo G. Silver, "Problems in Nineteenth-Century American Bibliography," in *The Bibliographical Society of America 1904-79: A Retrospective Collection* (Charlottesville, Va.: University Press of Virginia for the Bibliographical Society of America, 1980) pp. 126-38; Madeleine B. Stern, "The Role of the Publisher in Mid-Nineteenth-Century American Literature," *Publishing History* 10 (1981): [5]-26; Stuart Tipton Cooke, "Jacksonian Era American History Textbooks"

(Ph.D. diss., University of Denver, 1986), pp. 48-52; Ronald J. Zboray, "The Transportation Revolution and Antebellum Book Distribution Reconsidered," *American Quarterly* 38 (Spring 1986): [53]-71; Ronald J. Zboray, "Antebellum Reading and the Ironies of Technological Innovation," *American Quarterly* 40 (March 1988): 65-82. The latter article was part of a "Special Issue: Reading America," ed. Cathy N. Davidson. For some contemporary accounts, see Lossing, *American Centenary* (Philadelphia: Porter & Coates, 1876) pp. 475-79; *Trubner's Bibliographical Guide to American Literature*, comp. and ed. Nicolas Trubner (London: Trubner and Co., 1859), pp. xci, ci. Interest in the nineteenth-century literary marketplace represents a burgeoning field in cultural history. Among theoretical and methodological writings, I used Russell A. Berman, *Modern Culture and Critical Theory: Art, Politics, and the Legacy of the Frankfurt School* (Madison and London: The University of Wisconsin Press, 1989), especially pp. 54-69; Jean-Christophe Agnew, *Worlds Apart: The Market and the Theater in Anglo-American Thought, 1550-1750* (New Haven: Yale University Press, 1986); and a review essay, Roger D. Abrahams, "The Discovery of Marketplace Culture," *Intellectual History Newsletter* 10 (April 1988): 23-32.

2. Sources that elucidated this and other themes included: William Charvat, *Literary Publishing in America, 1790-1850* (Philadelphia: University of Pennsylvania Press, 1959); Cathy N. Davidson, "Books in the 'Good Old Days': A Portrait of the Early American Book Industry," *Book Research Quarterly* 2 (Winter 1986-87): 33-64; Michael T. Gilmore, *American Romanticism and the Marketplace* (Chicago: University of Chicago Press, 1985); R. Jackson Wilson, *Figures of Speech: American Writers and the Literary Marketplace, from Benjamin Franklin to Emily Dickinson* (New York: Alfred A. Knopf, 1989).

3. George Grote to Christiana M. Gibson, 17 September 1856, Gibson Scrapbook, Perkins Library, Duke University. See also Griffith J. McRee to David Swain, 12 March 1857, Swain Papers, Southern Historical Collection, University of North Carolina, Chapel Hill.

4. "Editorial Notes. American Literature and Reprints," *Putnam's* 8 (November 1856): 536-37; quotation on p. 537. See also "T. W. M.," "Signs of the Times," *American Publishers' Circular and Literary Gazette* 2 (24 May 1856): 302-3. A different perspective appeared in "Extracts from New Books. Bookselling—from Appleton's 'New American Cyclopaedia,'" *American Publishers' Circular and Literary Gazette* 4 (14 August 1858): 391. See also "Caesariensis," "Many Books," *Home Journal* 16 February 1850, p. 4 col. 3, which that periodical labeled as from the *Newark Daily Advertiser*.

5. In 1840, the *Telegraph* contained many examples of this practice. The 8 January issue (p. 1 col. 3-5) offered an essay and engraving relating to Oliver Cromwell that also appeared in the *Casket*. An eight-part series on the "Romance of History" that Lossing wrote for *The Family Magazine* appeared between 1 April and 2 December 1840, although by August these had become so sporadic that the paper began misnumbering them.

6. "L.," "Biography. David Hosack, M.D.F.R.S.," *Casket* 1 (16 January 1836): 13-14.

7. "Biography [Raleigh]," Ibid. 2 (29 December 1838): 145-46; quotation from p. 146.

8. "Biography. The Rajan Rammohun Roy," Ibid. 2 (23 March 1839): 193. Many nineteenth-century American intellectuals found Roy an appealing figure, although most did not join Lossing in counting the Indian thinker as an orthodox Christian. An

1818 *North American Review* article, for instance, concluded that Roy was not a Christian, although the writer thought he came near the faith on moral and theological points. "Miscellaneous Journal. Theology of the Hindoos, as taught by Ram Mohun Roy," *North American Review* 6 (March 1818): 393. See also Alan D. Hodder, "Emerson, Rammohan Roy, and the Unitarians," in *Studies in the American Renaissance 1988*, ed. Joel Myerson (Charlottesville: The University Press of Virginia, 1988) pp. 133-48.

9. "Zeta," "English History—Oliver Cromwell," *Casket* (28 December 1839): 145-46. "Oliver Cromwell," Ibid., 151.

10. "Original Miscellany. Architecture," Ibid. 1 (21 May 1836): 84. Elsewhere Lossing categorized music among the fine arts, a practice he did not continue in later publications. "Music and Musical Instruments," Ibid. 2 (3 November 1838): 116.

11. "Architecture in its earliest Stage," Ibid. 4 (22 August 1840: 73; "Architecture," Ibid. (19 September 1840): 89; "Architecture," and "Sculpture," Ibid. (3 October 1840): 97.

12. A source on these publications was Frank Luther Mott, *A History of American Magazines 1741-1850* (New York and London: D. Appleton and Company, 1930), pp. 363-65. Besides the journal with which Lossing was associated, another example was *The American Magazine of Useful and Entertaining Knowledge*, 3 vols. (Boston: Boston Bewick Co. [et al.], 1834-1837). In an 1841 list of "New Periodicals," four of seven magazines fell into this category. "Quarterly List of New Publications," *North American Review* 53 (October 1841): 543.

13. Lossing, *The American Centenary* (Philadelphia: Porter & Coates, 1876), p. 520; Lossing to R. Sheldon MacKenzie, 9 November 1876, Lossing Manuscripts, Historical Society of Pennsylvania. A sketch of Redfield in *The National Cyclopaedia of American Biography* (New York: James T. White & Co., 1897) VII: 188, included the same idea. In later years, Lossing tried to establish more facts about the *Magazine*, but by that time the seventy-year old Redfield could not remember much. The 1876 letter cited above was important on this point, as was J. Redfield to Lossing 3 October 1881, LS 1749, Lossing Addenda Box 21, Lossing Collection, Huntington Library.

14. "Poughkeepsie, Dutchess County, N.Y.," *Family Magazine* 6 (1838-39): 240-45. An Adams engraving, "The Last Arrow," appeared in the same volume, facing p. 120.

15. "Preface," *Family Magazine*, p. v.

16. "Christopher Columbus," Ibid., p. [3]. A few pages later Lossing included a poem on "Chivalry," in which he waxed eloquent on his enthusiasm for historical topics: "I joy to give my fancy rein, nor curb its airy flight,/ When to the buried Past it turns, and wanders 'mid the night/. . . ." Ibid., p. 12.

17. "Romance of History [I.]," Ibid., pp. 52-57; quotations from pp. 54 and 55.

18. "Romance of History.—No. VI. The League of Rutli," Ibid., p. 338.

19. Union catalogs and biographical sketches suggest these dates for editions of the *Outline History*: 1840, 1841, 1842, 1845, 1854, 1857, 1860, and 1868. A compilation of "Modern Works on Fine Arts," *Publishers' Weekly* 7 (30 January 1875): 108, referred to a new edition, but I have no other information on it. The copy I used was dated 1840, but some advertisements in the back of the book listed a book about the Mexican War, which suggests Harpers might have printed it around 1847.

20. A helpful source on the firm's early history was Howard C. Horsford's article in *American Literary Publishing Houses, 1638-1899 Part 1: A-M*, ed. Peter Dzwonkoski, Vol. 49 of *Dictionary of Literary Biography* (Detroit: Gale Research Company, 1986)

pp. 192-98. See also J. Henry Harper, *The House of Harper: A Century of Publishing in Franklin Square* (New York and London: Harper & Brothers, 1912); and, among nineteenth-century accounts, Lossing, *American Centenary,* pp. 506-9 and [Jacob Abbott], *The Harper Establishment; or, How the Story Books Are Made* (orig. ed. 1855; reprint Hamden, Conn.: The Shoe String Press, 1956).

21. As Lossing and others advocated in the 1830s, New York Public School District Libraries began functioning like public libraries; the Harpers series was one effort to profit from this new market. See Marilyn Haas, "New York's School District Library Movement and Harper's School District Library Books, 1839-1846," Paper presented at "Reading in America, 1840-1940, a Symposium," 22 November 1986, Strong Museum, Rochester. Thanks are due Ms. Haas for a copy of her paper.

22. "Literary Notices," *American Museum of Literature and the Arts* 1 (September 1838): 149. See also "The Philosophy of History," *North American Review* 39 (July 1834): 30-56, especially p. 56; and "The Messrs. Harpers' Publishing Establishment," *Morris's National Press. A Journal for Home* [later *Home Journal*] 18 April 1846, p. 2 col. 4-6; "Literary Notices," *New-York Mirror* 17 (16 May 1840): 375. Among more positive references, see "Literary Notices," *The Boston Miscellany* 3 (February 1843): 95; and especially "Notices of New Works," *Southern Literary Messenger* 9 (May 1843): 320.

23. Eugene Exman, *The Brothers Harper: A Unique Publishing Partnership and its Impact upon the Cultural Life of America from 1817 to 1853* (New York: Harper & Row, 1965) quoted Lossing without reference on pp. 125-26.

24. Ibid., 126.

25. An early example was [Mrs. Hannah F. Lee (Sawyer)], *Historical Sketches of the Old Painters* (Boston: Hilliard, Gray, & Co., 1838). Later significant contributions included several books by Charles C. Perkins of Massachusetts, such as *Tuscan Sculptors,* 2 vols (London: Longman, Green, Longman, Roberts, & Green, 1864); *Raphael and Michael Angelo* (Boston: J. R. Osgood and Company, 1878).

26. An invaluable source for the following paragraphs was Neil Harris, *The Artist in American Society: The Formative Years 1790-1860* ([New York]: Simon and Schuster, 1966). A cogent primary source was Samuel Lorenzo Knapp, *Lectures on American Literature* (orig. ed. 1829), reprinted as *American Cultural History 1607-1829* (Delmar, N.Y.: Scholars' Facsimiles & Reprints, 1977), pp. 190-208. See also Joseph Hopkinson, "The Fine Arts," in *The Philadelphia Book: or Specimens of Metropolitan Literature* (Philadelphia: Key & Biddle, 1836), pp. 79-86.

27. "A.B.," "North America. Peculiarities. State of the Fine Arts. Painting," *Blackwood's Edinburgh Magazine* 16 (August 1824): 131.

28. Sources on Dunlap's ideas have included contemporary reviews of his *History of the Rise and Progress of the Arts of Design in the United States*, 2 vols. (New York: G. P. Scott and Co., 1834): *The American Quarterly Review* 17 (March 1835): 143-77; *North American Review* 41 (July 1835): 146-70. A later article also discussed that work: "The Fine Arts in America," *Southern Quarterly Review* 15 (July 1849): 333-55. Rembrandt Peale to C. Edwards Lester, 8 March 1846, quoted in Lester, *The Artists of America: A Series of Biographical Sketches of American Artists* (New York: Baker & Scribner, 1846), p. 200.

29. Both these quotations appeared in "The Fine Arts in America," *Southern Quarterly Review* 15 (July 1849): 336, 337. See also J. K. Fisher [of New York City], "Culture of the Fine Arts," *Southern Literary Messenger* 6 (December 1840): 842-46;

"The Influence of the Fine Arts on the National Character," *Southern Literary Messenger* 30 (March 1860): 202-9.

30. C. D. Stuart, "American Fine Arts and Artists," *The Republic* 1 (June 1851): 259-62; a contrasting view appeared in "The American School of Art," *The American Whig Review* 16 [new series 10] (August 1852): 138-48. See also "F.A.P.," "Modern Art.—Powers' Statue of Calhoun," *Southern Quarterly Review* 21 [n.s. 6] (January 1852): 86-114.

31. "Literary Notices," *The New-York Mirror* 18 (27 June 1840): 7.

32. *The New York Review* 7 (July 1840): 251-52.

4

A CAREER REVIVED: 1841–1848

Although Lossing's works from the 1840s have mostly remained obscure, this decade held great significance for his career. First, he solidified his standing as an engraver. More importantly for his writing career, the late 1840s witnessed his first book-length excursions into American history. Those endeavors gave him opportunities to celebrate what he perceived as America's special place in historical progress. His success revived his career and laid a foundation for future triumphs.

The failure of Lossing's first book, the *Outline History of the Fine Arts*, led to several years of writing inactivity. Through the early 1840s, he devoted more attention to his engraving business. But even in this capacity, Lossing remained conscious of the literary marketplace, because books and magazines represented the major outlets for his illustrations. Before decade's end, his connections with New York publishers would give Lossing opportunities to again enter the sphere of historical authorship; this time with a consistent emphasis on American topics. Unlike the *Outline History*, his works in this new field proved commercially and intellectually satisfying. His career's revival requires discussion, because it set the stage for his first great work, *The Pictorial Field-Book of the Revolution*.

While Lossing had undertaken several literary projects by this time, his fame still came from wood-engraving. One *Poughkeepsie Casket* contributor, for instance, referred to him as "a well[-]known wood engraver."[1] Lossing was most active in the engraving business he founded around 1839; it later became the Lossing-Barritt company. That firm was an important facet of Lossing's career through the 1860s. It gave him a relatively steady income, so that he could risk time and money on writing history books. It helped Lossing establish contacts with writers and publishers that brought him to the literary industry's core. As a co-partner in a business that employed various journeyman engravers, Lossing did not have a hand in every illustration that bore a "Lossing" or "Lossing-Barritt" label, but this label's appearance in many contemporary books and magazines suggested the role he and his colleagues played in New York's illustration market.[2]

In 1842, a letter revealed Lossing's knowledge of New York's engraving market. Responding to inquiries from a prospective engraver who had sent samples of his work, Lossing judged that "these specimens show much skill, especially when your disadvantages are considered." But, he continued, with any of several possible motives, "the profession is already too full here to make this city an eligible place for a beginner." "Several English and French Engravers have arrived here within a year, ready to work at any price," he explained, "and producing a good deal of competition. The consequence is, that some of our native artists are, some of the time, without work." Still, Lossing offered to help his neophyte friend in any way possible if he came to New York.[3]

This document was significant for two reasons. First, it showed that individuals outside the metropolis knew Lossing as an engraver and valued his opinions about their capability to enter the field successfully. Second, they recognized that, so far as market questions went, he possessed special insight on New York. Over the next few years, this knowledge grew more extensive as Lossing undertook illustration projects for various publishers. In two cases, Harper & Brothers and Edward Walker, Lossing's work for specific publishers was important—not just for his illustration business but because after he re-entered literary work, these houses published several of his books.

As we have seen, the *Outline History of the Fine Arts* (1840) represented an unpleasant experience for Lossing and Harper & Brothers. But the firm did not let this failure affect engraving contracts with Lossing. In August 1845, Lossing agreed to supply over 1,200 wood-cuts for a four-volume *Pictorial History of England*. The contract specified that Lossing's firm would complete these within two years, and he met this deadline.[4]

The *Pictorial History* was the work of several British writers, with George L. Craik and Charles MacFarlane producing most of its contents. Its precise impact on Lossing's career as "a pictorial author" is impossible to gauge; but these volumes' similarity to his most important books of the 1850s and 1860s is striking.[5] Nor is such a remark simply a product of hindsight, because reviewers expressed awareness that its emphasis on "pictorial representations" represented a break with conventional historical composition. One columnist characterized the *Pictorial History* as "picturesque" in stressing artifacts and locales as much as events. The work "is one among the numerous evidences of a great change that has been going on, of late years, in historical composition. History is no longer a mere compendium of battles and sieges, . . . but a mirror in which all the minute particulars of past ages are accurately reflected."[6]

Harper and Brothers found Lossing's work for the *Pictorial History* acceptable, and soon they gave him more contracts. For Lossing's career, the most important contract came with the *Pictorial Field-Book of the Revolution*. But before that opus started Lossing's mature career, his engraving work for another publisher, Edward Walker, had more immediate significance for reinitiating Lossing's historical writing.[7]

From 1845 through the mid-1850s, Lossing supplied hundreds of engravings for Walker. One of his earlier projects was to illustrate Baptist pastor John Dowling's polemic *History of Romanism* that, within a decade, sold around 25,000 copies. Protestant editors trumpeted the *History* as a "great work," and contemporary anti-Catholic agitation found vivid reflection in its pages. One scholar inferred from his involvement with this book that Lossing, too, had nativistic sentiments.[8] But a paucity of evidence leaves uncertain the degree to which Lossing acted out of conviction or commercial interest, or both.

In 1847, Walker approached Lossing about writing a history of the American Revolution. Within weeks Lossing was using spare moments to write this narrative. Soon Walker published Lossing's manuscript as *Seventeen Hundred and Seventy-six, or, The War of Independence . . . .*; they continued printing new editions over the next five years.[9]

The significance of *Seventeen Hundred and Seventy-six* for Lossing's career resists facile definition. We do not know how many copies Walker sold, although his decision to issue several editions suggests he found it profitable. Contemporary magazine and newspaper reviews were overwhelmingly positive. Thus it seems likely that the success of this first extended venture into American history encouraged Lossing to believe he had found a literary field that fit his talents and disposition. This realization was important for a writer smarting from the failure of an earlier, more ambitious book.

In writing a work on the Revolutionary War, Lossing sought to benefit from public interest in that topic, and in military history, generally. "Military histories were never more generally and eagerly read than in this century," one writer commented in 1848, partly because of the contemporary conflict with Mexico.[10] Nationalism, expressed in many Americans' sense of pride in national accomplishments, further encouraged such writings, giving "national history," in the words of William G. Simms, attributes of "a national religion."[11]

American writings specifically on the War for Independence already represented a voluminous and rapidly expanding literature. In the first decades after the United States won their independence, historians of the Revolution—including Mercy Otis Warren, David Ramsay, and Benjamin Trumbull—anticipated later scholars in various ways. They justified the Patriots' "rebellion" as a laudable protest against British tyranny. They presented the Revolution as part of God's Providential plan for bringing liberty to the world.[12] Later, that viewpoint found its most memorable expression in George Bancroft's vast *History of the United States*. But when Lossing wrote *Seventeen Hundred and Seventy-six*, Bancroft had not yet reached the Revolution, so his influence on that book was minimal.[13] As a discussion of illustrations for his book will demonstrate, Lossing's models came from less exalted sources.

Lossing's introduction covered both conventional and original ground. Comments about the book's illustrations touched upon some themes that remained important throughout his career. Lossing maintained that he included pictures in his book "not merely for the purpose of attracting the popular eye, without reference to fitness or meaning; they are illustrative of facts, and form a part of the record." The engravings were accurate because he based them on personal research. "The delineations of Interesting Localities, having Revolutionary associations clustered around them, may be relied on as correct, all of them having been drawn by the writer, either from nature, or from approved pictures. The Portraits, likewise . . . , have been carefully copied from engravings which enjoy the public approval" (p. [x]).

From what sources did Lossing formulate the practice of using engravings to convey information? The issue is significant, because Lossing soon carried the idea into the *Pictorial Field-Book*, a work which embodied his best gifts as a historian. Probably Harper's *Pictorial History of England*, for which he had supplied pictures, had some influence. Another model could have been the example of Robert Sears, a Canadian then writing and publishing in New York.[14]

One scholar has suggested that the historical popularizer John Frost served as Lossing's most important model. Frost, despite teaching and administrative duties in a Philadelphia high school, produced biographies and "Pictorial Histories" on various topics through this period. Besides a lack of documentation, the main problem with linking Frost to Lossing is that in Frost's books and those of similar writers, most pictures played precisely the role Lossing sought to avoid; they were decorations or "embellishments" with no informational content. It seems unlikely that Frost influenced Lossing, except in presenting practices Lossing wanted to avoid.[15]

A better candidate as Lossing's intellectual precursor was John Warner Barber (1798-1885), a Connecticut engraver and antiquarian. Barber, like Lossing, received early training in illustration. In the 1830s, Barber began traveling through his native state, and later roamed other regions in New England and beyond. He collected oral and documentary sources related to each state's history, corresponded with antiquarians, and consulted published materials. He illustrated his books with wood engravings through which he sought to record historical information. In 1838, Lossing's *Poughkeepsie Casket* included extracts from one of these volumes, indicating Lossing's familiarity with Barber. Although we cannot prove Barber's influence on Lossing, his work had more in common with Lossing's *Field-Books* than any other writer.[16]

Seventeen Hundred and Seventy-six presented a contrast between the British and Americans that made the Revolutionary War "emphatically a war of Principle; a conflict of Opinion and for Power, between Despotism and Freedom; a struggle of the patrician few with the plebeian many for the mastery"(p. [17]). The conflict's outcome fit well with God's plan for human progress. "The ways of a mysterious Providence were made plain; a mighty problem was solved; a brighter morning than earth ever saw, . . . dawned upon humanity, and the car of progress, so long inert, started upon its wondrous course" (p. 19).

The Revolution as a turning point in history dominated Lossing's larger interpretation. Even Europe benefitted because the war "taught monarchs and statesmen a great moral lesson, . . . to respect the inalienable rights of the governed, and to regard political freedom as the firmest pillar of the throne" (p. 20). Ironically, America's best student was the power from which it had revolted. "Britain, though old, has been an apt scholar in learning the lesson taught by our War of Independence, and nobly are her children practising its precepts. Monarchy there is now but a dim shadow of its former self" (p. 23).

To elucidate the Revolution's significance, Lossing sought its roots in earlier events. He recorded how, for over a century after 1651, English commercial laws affecting the colonies—especially the various Navigation Acts—"were really oppressive and unjust in the extreme" (p. 53). Some royal governors, only too willing to cooperate with such oppression, advocated plans of union out of "mercenary" motives. They sought to further the crown's powers and check, "in its incipient growth, the budding spirit of independence, becoming so frequently manifest." Unwise imperial efforts to crush the Americans' love of liberty ironically "gave new life to languishing aspirations for freedom" (p. 26).

The late colonial period deepened American disenchantment with the British when they proved unable to exploit advantages over their French rivals. When, in 1748, the British returned Louisbourg to New France, resentment over this action "weakened the loyalty of the Colonies, and awakened a spirit of discontent, deep and permanent" (p. 30). The climactic French and Indian War (1754-1763) proved again to Americans that the British were not competent to rule or defend their country. That conflict also made colonists aware of their own future leaders, especially George Washington. This perception, in Lossing's view, enjoyed Providential endorsement. He claimed to find signs of Divine favor when he recalled that Washington had been the only mounted Anglo-American officer to escape injury in one battle" (p. 36).

After the defeat of France, the new fiscal demands placed on the colonies by the King and Parliament only made discontent more evident. Great Britain should have appreciated its colonies' contribution to the Empire's strength.

But her avarice and ambition too often filmed her vision to her true interests; and this political blindness led her into the monstrous error of oppressing her children; children who regarded her with affection and reverence, and who never dreamed of leaving the paternal roof, until the unholy chastisements of a parent's hand alienated their love, expelled them from the threshold, and compelled them to seek shelter and security behind the bulwarks of a righteous rebellion (pp. 49-50).

Lossing stressed the Revolution's early years (1763-1770) as a high point for all history, "a period to which the annalists of the Past pointed prospectively with hopeful aspirations; and towards which the chroniclers of the Future will look retrospectively with grateful benedictions upon their lips" (p. [51]). He claimed to discern a process of imperial oppression through these years that became explicit in the 1763 Stamp Act, and continued to grow through the imperial Writs of Assistance, judicial documents that let British judges rule on colonial cases. "These events caused the colonists to ponder seriously; and their minds were opened, perhaps for the first time, to the importance of a state of Independence" (p. 54). Only one year later, Lossing averred, the Americans found themselves upholding a "fundamental principle—'TAXATION AND REPRESENTATION ARE INSEPARABLE'" (p. 57).

Lossing's narrative of the Revolutionary War included many derisive comments on English conduct. When, early in the war, the British offered to pardon Americans who deserted to their side, Lossing remarked that the overture represented an "olive branch . . . disfigured by parasites of royal growth" (p. 201). Lossing found the British use of Hessian mercenary troops odious. Within two years of the conflict's start, Lossing noted, the atrocities committed by British and Hessian troops pushed even many Loyalists into the patriot ranks (pp. 186, 221).

Contrasts with the British grew evident as Lossing chronicled the character and actions of patriot soldiers, commanders, and even, to a lesser degree, politicians. The Continental Army's suffering at Valley Forge, for Lossing, had no precedent; here was the epitome of selfless, sacrificial virtue. Their sacrifice loomed larger as Lossing considered the range of problems they confronted. "Yet amidst all this suffering day after day, surrounded by frost and snow, patriotism was still warm and hopeful in the hearts of the soldiers, and the love of self was merged into the one great sentiment, *love of country*" (p. 252).

Among patriot generals, Washington naturally held a preeminent position, although Lossing esteemed him as much for political as military acumen. Washington's moral stature grew manifest as American resolve flagged in 1776. "It was a gloomy hour for America, . . . Yet that immortal man stood up amidst these despondencies, like a firm tower of strength, and, leaning upon the arm of that Providence which had so signally protected him in times past, he felt confident of success, for he knew the cause was a righteous one" (p. 217).

Washington's friendship with LaFayette generated enough patriotic glory to make familiarity with each man's life a prerequisite for true republican citizenship. "The names of Washington and LaFayette are so inseparably connected, that it seems to be a sort of treason against the just laws of patriotic sentiment for any American to be ignorant of the life of either" (p. 227n). Here was a rationale for historical study that made it fundamental to full participation in national life.

Lossing's conclusion contrasted the righteous American cause with those of other revolutions. He did not specifically mention the French Revolution, but it remained his implicit negative example. "Unlike the revolutions of other times, whose conception and execution were frequently simultaneous, and when physical power, aided only by the inflammatory harangues, or promised benefits, of demagogues, supported rebellion, and overturned existing government," he wrote, "our Revolution was the result of long years of patiently-endured oppression—of violated principles, whose unfettered exercise is an essential element of human freedom" (pp. 367-368).

Seventeen Hundred and Seventy-six received many favorable newspaper and magazine reviews. Walker, anxious to exploit these, reprinted selections from the notices in several places, including other books and his edition of a British magazine.[17]

This document conveniently summarized many responses to Lossing's book, although it is important to recall its promotional intent.

Several reviews commented on Lossing as a talented historical writer. *The Merchants' Magazine* found his "chaste and graceful" prose notable, especially since he was also "an engraver of more than ordinary skill[.]" A *New York Express* writer thought that Lossing's book "cannot fail to give him an enviable reputation as an historian." *The Farmer and Mechanic* maintained that "the *style* of the work is a *model* for history, and an honorable illustration of the refinement of intellectual power, which is being developed in this country, in connexion [sic] with the exercise of practical mechanics and the arts."[18]

Others commended Lossing for including reprints of documents from the Revolution. Nearly always these reviewers mentioned that, as the *Knickerbocker Magazine* put it, these were papers "that the present generation are but slightly familiar with[.]" Some notices stressed the need for the nation's young generation to study the Revolution, something that, in their estimation, rendered Lossing's book "the most appropriate gift of which we know, for presentation to an American youth; and it is one which should be studied well and often by every American youth."[19]

Seventeen Hundred and Seventy-six represented a turning point in Lossing's career. For the first time, he had written an extended historical work that won critical acclaim. This book gave Lossing a topic—the

American Revolution—for which he possessed talent and enthusiasm. With this experience as encouragement, he pressed on to solidify his standing as a historian, first through minor works and then in the monumental *Field-Book of the Revolution*.

For unclear reasons, Lossing's next publications were not issued by Edward Walker, although Lossing continued to prepare illustrations for Walker. Lossing's next books evidenced Lossing's attempts to extend the success of *Seventeen Hundred and Seventy-six* into other American historical and biographical topics. Their obscurity and lack of originality suggest that his efforts did not win substantive rewards.

The first book consisted of brief biographies of American presidents. H. Phelps & Co. published the work in late 1847, and printed later editions before other publishers obtained its rights. In preparing this work, Lossing may have used antecedent books of American and foreign writers, and he probably did not expend much effort on it.[20]

The most interest this book generated was for its preface, in which Lossing mentioned his aim "of presenting in a popular form, for the instruction of youthful Americans," chapters on the presidents' characters and careers. He also announced plans for more books along those lines. "This is the first of a series of works, adapted to the tastes and wants of the young American, which we intend to prepare for the press, under the earnest impression that in this way germs of knowledge, particularly useful to the American citizen, may be from time to time implanted in the luxuriant soil of the popular mind, that will, in the future, spring up and bring forth fruit a thousand-fold."[21]

An atmosphere of modest but earnest educational endeavor persisted as Lossing described his role in this venture. "[W]e shall gladly perform the duty of usher at the portals of popular intelligence, pointing like a guide-post to the spacious galleries within: for we had rather be a door-keeper in the house of wisdom than to dwell in the tents of ignorance." Introducing a derivative, soon-forgotten book, Lossing was offering to serve the American public as a self-conscious historical popularizer. In many ways, the remainder of his career involved attempts to fulfill this promise.

Lossing next wrote a volume on the Declaration of Independence and its signers. G. F. Cooledge & Brother of New York published the *Signers* book in the spring of 1848; in the 1850s and later, other firms in various cities reissued it. Possibly Lossing moved to other publishers because he was dissatisfied with the physical make-up of Cooledge's books; at least, one of his readers expressed displeasure on this point. "I have just met with your book about the Signers of the General Declaration of Independence," this antiquarian wrote, commenting that he perused it "with avidity for it was just the book I have been wanting for a long time." He added, however, that "[i]t is worthy of a better dress than *Cooledge* has given it."[22]

In writing about the Declaration, Lossing connected with a rich tradition of pictorial and literary expression; the Declaration held such resonance with many Americans that, even more than the Constitution, they looked upon it as a foundational document for their society's values and norms. Benjamin Trumbull's painting of the document's signing became one of the most popular reproductions of the period, and many engravers circulated copies of the Declaration. Especially after 1820, collective biographies of the signers appeared often and could have served as sources for Lossing.[23]

The book with which *Signers* had the most in common was a late 1820s tome by Charles A. Goodrich. The brother of children's author Samuel G. Goodrich, himself a writer of several American history schoolbooks, Charles Goodrich anticipated Lossing in depicting the signers as God's instruments for achieving the nation's independence and hence furthering liberty for humankind.[24] Indeed, as Lossing cited virtues of the Revolutionary generation, he often came close to plagiarizing the earlier biographer's words.

Lossing's final project before the *Field-Book of the Revolution* both recalled earlier writings and anticipated later ones. Through 1848, Lossing edited *The Young People's Mirror*, a juvenile monthly, published by Edward Walker. The *Mirror*, which only survived for a year, had much in common with *The Family Magazine* of a decade before and even with the *Poughkeepsie Casket*. One theme that persisted from *The Family Magazine* was Lossing's interest in the contemporary journalism. An essay on "The Press" encouraged newspaper and magazine writers to recognize their crucial role in society, especially in making the public aware of history and its lessons. "Through you Past Generations speak to the Present, and lips that have been mummied for thirty centuries, whisper their lessons of wisdom in the ears of even the little children of our day. You are the great schoolmasters of the nations."[25]

Some readers' responses to the *Mirror* have survived, with most expressing positive reactions. One reader enthused that he would "have no hesitancy in pronouncing it the Best Periodical at the price that I have ever seen[.]"[26] The extent to which such comments encouraged Lossing to new endeavors is difficult to measure, but at this time he was developing original ideas about researching and writing history. The *Mirror* contained hints along these lines. One issue included a letter that Lossing wrote from Burlington, Vermont, to Walker. Here he described his plan to visit sites of the French and Indian War and the Revolution.[27]

An editorial on the "Ingratitude of Republics" articulated a rationale for such research. Decrying the lack of public or private interest in funding monuments to the nation's past, Lossing remarked that "[w]ithin the last few months we have visited many of the battle-fields and other interesting localities of our Revolution, yet nowhere have we yet seen a monument erected by Congress, either upon the grounds where our fathers contended for freedom, or over the ashes of those who led them to battle." Lossing's conclusion implied that his work might rectify this situation if young Americans imbibed proper lessons from it. "We hope the young, now coming upon the stage of active life, will cultivate a more patriotic spirit, and . . . endeavor to wrest from utter oblivion, these sacred spots."[28]

To realize this goal, Lossing undertook travels for two years that covered 9,000 miles. The resulting two-volume work, *The Pictorial Field-Book of the Revolution*, laid the foundation for his remaining career and, for over a quarter-century, remained one of the most popular works on the nation's founding. That journey, which in one sense never ended during Lossing's life, began innocently enough in June 1848, as he traveled along a quiet Connecticut road.

NOTES

1. "Enigma," *Casket* 3 (4 April 1840): 205.

2. W. L. Burroughs to Elihu Geer, 22 June 1842, Book Trades Collection, American Antiquarian Society, Box 2, Folder 14.

3. Lossing to "Mr. Beadle," 29 October 1842, Beadle Family Manuscripts, New York Public Library.

4. Lossing contract with Harper & Brothers, 25 August 1845, Harpers Archives, Correspondence Relating to Contracts Box 18, Columbia University Special Collections Library. I read this in the microfilm edition of this collection, reel 53.

5. On Craik (1798-1866), see the article in *Dictionary of National Biography* (London: Humphrey Milford, 1937-1938), V: 1-2. Harpers' publication of the *History*'s four-volume American edition spanned the years 1846-1851. They also published some of his books in the Family Library and other series. On Lossing as a "pictorial author," see J. C. Derby, *Fifty Years Among Authors—Books and Publishers* [sic] New York: G. W. Carleton & Co., 1884), p. 686.

6. "Notices of New Works," *Southern Literary Messenger* 13 (February 1847): 128; *Southern Quarterly Review* 10 (July 1846): 253; "Notices of New Works," *Southern Literary Messenger* 14 (May 1848): 329-30; the quotations in this paragraph and the next from p. 330.

7. I based this upon advertisements in Lossing, *Seventeen Hundred and Seventy-six* (New York: Edward Walker, 1847).

8. On Dowling (1807-1878), see Allibone, *Dictionary*, I: 516-517 and a sketch in *The National Cyclopaedia of American Biography* (New York: James T. White & Co., 1907), IX: 216. The latter source listed the *Romanism* book's sales at 30,000. The "great work" quotation was from "Critical Notices," *The Biblical Repository and Classical Review*, 3rd ser. 5 (April 1849): 378. On this project as a reflection of Lossing's views, see Diane M. Casey, "Benson Lossing: His Life and Work, 1830-1860," *Syracuse University Library Associates Courier* 20 (Spring 1985): 84-86.

9. Union catalogs suggested editions in 1847, 1848, 1849, 1850, 1852.

10. "Critical Notices," *Southern Quarterly Review* 14 (July 1848): 242.

11. Simms, "History for the Purposes of Art," in his *Views and Reviews in American Literature, History and Fiction, First Series* (New York: Wiley and Putnam, 1845), pp. 36, 40.

12. Secondary sources on these writers included: Wesley Frank Craven, *The Legend of the Founding Fathers* (New York: New York University Press, 1956); William R. Smith, *History as Argument: Three Patriot Historians of the American Revolution* (The Hague: Mouton, 1966); *The Colonial Legacy: Early Nationalist Historians* (New York: Harper & Row, 1973); Arthur H. Shaffer, *The Politics of History: Writing the History of the American Revolution, 1783-1815* (Chicago: Precedent Publishing, 1975). See also Lawrence J. Friedman and Arthur H. Shaffer, "Mercy Otis Warren and the Politics of Historical Nationalism," *New England Quarterly* 48 (June 1975): 194-215; Friedman and Shaffer, "David Ramsay and the Quest for an American Historical Identity," *Southern Quarterly* 14 (July 1976): 351-71.

13. Contemporary sources on Bancroft were numerous. See "Continuation of Bancroft's History," *North American Review* 74 (April 1852): 507-15; "Bancroft," *Putnam's* 1 (March 1853): 300-8; "George Bancroft," *The National Magazine* 6 (January 1855): 67-72; "Mr. Bancroft's Mode of Writing History," *National Quarterly Review* 25 (December 1874): 80-92. Secondary accounts I found helpful included: Watt Stewart, "George Bancroft," in *The Marcus W. Jernegan Essays in American Historiography*, ed. William T. Hutchinson (New York: Russell and Russell, 1937), pp. 1-24; Russel B. Nye, *George Bancroft: Brahmin Rebel* (New York: Knopf, 1944); Robert H. Canary, *George Bancroft* in *Twayne's United States Authors Series* No. 266 (New York: Twayne Publishers, Inc., 1974); Lilian Handlin, *George Bancroft: The Intellectual as Democrat* (New York [et. al.]: Harper & Row, 1984).

14. In American history, Sears's most important work was *A New Pictorial Description of the United States* (New York: Robert Sears, 1848 and later editions). See Allibone, *Dictionary*, II: 1985; and William Bristol Shaw's article in *Dictionary of American Biography*, ed. Dumas Malone (New York: Charles Scribner's Sons, 1935), VIII: 541.

15. Robert W. Johannsen, *To the Halls of the Montezumas: The Mexican War in the American Imagination* (New York and Oxford: Oxford University Press, 1985), pp. 223, 260-61. "Critical Notices," *The American Review: A Whig Journal* 5 (May 1847): 542. Earlier sources on Frost included: Allibone, *Dictionary*, I: 639-40; *Herringshaw's Encyclopedia of American Biography of the Nineteenth Century,* ed. Thomas William Herringshaw (Chicago: American Publishers' Association, 1905), p. 384. One of Frost's most popular books was *The Wonders of History* (New York: Cornish, Lamport & Co., 1851). A similar use of illustrations appeared in R. Thomas, *A Pictorial History of the United States of America* (Hartford: House & Brown, 1848).

16. "Miscellany. Auld Lang Syne," *Casket* 2 (14 July 1838): 53. On Barber, see Richard Hegel, *Nineteenth-Century Historians of New Haven* (Hamden, Conn.: Archon Books, 1972), pp. 32-50; and Hegel, "John Warner Barber," in *American Historians, 1607-1865*, ed. Clyde N. Wilson, Vol. 30 of *Dictionary of Literary Biography* (Detroit: Gale Research Company, 1984), pp. 23-30. Some autobiographical material appeared in an introduction to Barber, *The Bible Looking Glass* (Philadelphia: Bradley, Garretson & Co. [et. al.], 1876), pp. [i]-iii.

17. I used the latter copy, Ms. 18081, New York State Library, Albany. The magazine in which this appeared was *Blackwood's Edinburgh Magazine. New American Edition* 25 (October 1847). The compilation's separate pagination was [1]-8.

18. *Merchants' Magazine*, September 1847, in *Blackwood's Edinburgh Magazine*, October 1847, p. 2; New York Express in *Blackwood's Edinburgh Magazine,* October 1847, p. 3. See also *Evening Mirror* quotation, *Blackwood's Edinburgh Magazine*

October 1847; *Farmer and Mechanic* in *Blackwood's Edinburgh Magazine*, p. 4; *New York Observer*, *Blackwood's Edinburgh Magazine*; *Augusta* [Georgia] *Chronicle & Sentinel*, *Blackwood's Edinburgh Magazine*, p. 7; *Albany Spectator*, *Blackwood's Edinburgh Magazine*, p. 4.

19. *Knickerbocker Magazine*, August 1847, *Blackwood's Edinburgh Magazine*, p. 2. See also, in Ibid., quotations from *The New York Observer*,p. 4; from Rochester, N.Y. *Daily Advertiser*, p. 6; from *Poughkeepsie Journal & Eagle*, p. 6; from the *Sunday Mercury*, p. 8. Notice from *Brooklyn Eagle* in *Blackwood's Edinburgh Magazine*, p. 5; see also reviews from: *Albany Spectator* on p. 4; *New Orleans Picayune*, p. 5.

20. The copy I consulted was of this first edition: Benson J. Lossing, *The Lives of the Presidents of the United States* (New York: H. Phelps & Co., 1847). Later editions included: (New York: H. Phelps & Co., 1848); (New York and Buffalo: Ensign & Thayer, 1849); (New York: Phelps & Fanning, 1851); (New York: Ensign, Bridgman, & Fanning, 1858). Examples of similar books included: Ignatius Loyola Robertson [sic], *Sketches of Public Characters* (New-York: E. Bliss [et. al.], 1830), pp. 63-81; Robert W. Lincoln, *Lives of the Presidents of the United States* (New York: Published for W. W. Reed, 1833) and later editions to 1853; Edwin Williams, *The Presidents of the United States, their Memoirs and Administrations* (New York: Edward Walker, 1849) and later editions; Henry C. Watson, *Lives of the Presidents of the United States* (Boston: Kelley & Brother, 1853); John Frost, *The Presidents of the United States* (Boston: Phillips, Sampson and Company, 1854) and later editions.

21. Lossing, *Lives of the Presidents*, p. [5].

22. The first edition was B. J. Lossing, *Biographical Sketches of the Signers of the Declaration of American Independence: The Declaration Historically Considered* (New York: G. F. Cooledge & Brother, 1848). The edition I read was (New York: J. C. Derby; Boston: Phillips, Sampson & Co.; Cincinnati: H. W. Derby, 1854). Later incarnations included: (Boston: John Philbrick, 1856); (New York: Derby & Jackson; Cincinnati: H. W. Derby & Co., 1857); (New York: Derby & Jackson, 1860); (Philadelphia: Davis, Porter & Co., 1866); (Philadelphia: Evans, Stoddart & Co., 1870). Charles Phillips to Lossing, 27 January 1852, Mecklenburg Declaration Papers, Southern Historical Collection, University of North Carolina, Chapel Hill.

23. On books and prints about the Declaration, see John Bidwell, "American History in Image and Text," *Proceedings of the American Antiquarian Society* 98 (1989): 247-302. Among books on the signers, the most voluminous entry was John Sanderson, *Biography of the Signers of the Declaration of Independence,* 9 Vols. (Philadelphia: R. W. Pomeroy, 1820-1827). A review of Sanderson's first two volumes appeared in the *North American Review* 16 (January 1823): 184-96. See also Samuel Lorenzo Knapp, *Lectures on American Literature* (orig. ed. 1829); reprinted as *American Cultural History 1607-1829* (Delmar, N.Y.: Scholars' Facsimiles & Reprints, 1977), p. 130. This vast work, which, according to Knapp, Sanderson only edited, appeared in various editions for fifty years. See also L. Carroll Judson, *A Biography of the Signers of the Declaration of Independence* (Philadelphia: J. Dobson, and Thomas, [sic] Cowperthwait & Co., 1839).

24. Goodrich, *Lives of the Signers of the Declaration of Independence; with a Sketch of the Life of Washington,* earliest edition 1829; the copy I read was a reprint of Hartford: H. E. Robins and Co., 1848.

25. "The Press," *Mirror* 1 (1 March 1848): 34.

26. N. B. Tompkins to Walker 1 January 1847 [sic; an error for 1848],; L. H. Shute to Walker, 14 January 1848, Manuscript Call No. 18081, New York State Library.

27. "My Dear Walker," *Mirror* 2 (1 September 1848): 36-37.

28. "Ingratitude of Republics," *Mirror* 2 (1 November 1848): 60.

5

FROM DAN TO BEERSHEBA: *THE PICTORIAL FIELD-BOOK OF THE REVOLUTION*

"The American is by nature locomotive," Virginian Henry T. Tuckerman observed around 1849, even as Benson Lossing was conducting research travels for his *Pictorial Field-Book of the Revolution*. "Restless, active, and inquiring—with the instinct of progress continually at work, Americans almost seem to exist by virtue of movement, as the orientals do by quiescence. Such an existence favors quickness of perception however inimical it may be to contemplative energy. Self-reliance leads to adventure." In the *Field-Book*, historical research became an adventure for Lossing and his readers.

An irony of Tuckerman's remarks for Lossing was that Tuckerman thought Americans wrote good travel literature because, unlike Europeans, they betrayed no fixation with history or traditions. "With no time-honored customs or strong local associations to bind him to the soil, with little hereditary dignity of name or position to sustain, and accustomed, from infancy, to witness frequent changes of position and fortune, the inhabitant of no civilized land has so little restraint upon his vagrant humor as a native of the United States."[1] But Lossing's project was to establish such "associations" for Americans, to give them a history not only familiar to their minds but foundational for their personal characters as it inspired them to healthy national pride. He sought to realize these aims by crafting an intensely personal document about his search for a usable national past.

The Field-Book, researched and written from 1848 to 1850 and published by Harper & Brothers first in thirty installments or "numbers" and then as two thick volumes in 1850-52 and later, represented Lossing's most famous contribution to historical writing. Through the rest of his career, the *Field-Book* was always the first work with which publishers and readers identified him. Long after it first appeared, a *Publishers' Weekly* poll found that

American publishers ranked it as "the most salable [sic]" work on its topic.[2] For decades, historians used the *Field-Book* and modeled their books upon it. Readers prized the opus as a mine of entertaining yet edifying reading. From this point, for many Americans, Lossing remained a "pictorial author," an identity he neither attempted nor wanted to dispel.[3]

Lossing's propensity for describing picturesque and significant locales made the *Field-Book* an example of a "local color school" of historiography. Clearly Lossing possessed a capacity for the laborious research and travel that such a project required, and friends expressed wonder at the hard work he devoted to it. Washington Irving commented that "I am surprised to find in how short a time you have accomplished your undertaking, considering you have had to travel from Dan to Beersheba to collect facts and anecdotes, sketch and engrave, write, print and correct the proofs, and with all this to have accomplished it in so satisfactory a manner."[4]

Lossing's accomplishment—probably the greatest of his life—sprang from a seemingly transitory incident in June 1848, as he traveled on horseback between Greenwich and Stamford, Connecticut. He noticed some stone steps that colonial workmen had cut. He asked an old man about them, and that "patriarch," a former militia officer, related how General Israel Putnam escaped from British troops in 1779, using those steps. Lossing recalled:

This incident and its associations made a deep impression on my mind. I had been brought suddenly into the presence of animate and inanimate relics of the old war for independence, both of which were fading away and soon to be seen no more on the earth forever. I felt an irrepressible desire to seek and find such mementoes of the great conflict for freedom and independence, wherever they might exist, and to snatch their lineaments from the grasp of Decay before it should be too late.[5]

In this way, the *Field-Book*'s germ sprang into Lossing's mind.

That night, Lossing drafted a plan for his project. He suggested to Harper & Brothers that with financial help he could visit Revolutionary sites in the United States and Canada and use descriptions of them as a springboard for tracing events at each locale. On July 17, 1848, the publishers agreed to Lossing's plan and issued a contract. This agreement recorded a working title for the one-volume work he and his publishers expected to produce: "A Pictorial and Descriptive Tour to the Historical Localities of the American Revolution[.]" Both writer and publisher estimated 300 engravings as necessary for the book.

Lossing recalled afterwards that work on the *Field-Book* took two years.[6] But Harper & Brothers did not finish actual publication until late 1852, more than two years after Lossing completed his chores. This suggests that Lossing's publishers faced problems in keeping pace with him. They recognized this difficulty as Lossing began traveling and gathering sketches, interviews, and documents.

In 1848 Lossing took five tours through the northern United States and lower Canada. First he visited the Upper Hudson Valley and the Saratoga-Ticonderoga region, then moved into Quebec, Montreal, and western New York before returning to New York City. Lossing's second trip (mid-September 1848) took him through New Jersey, Pennsylvania's historic Wyoming Valley, then back to New York. Late that same month he began a third journey, for which Boston and other Massachusetts cities served as the focus. In a fourth tour (October 1848), Lossing spent time in Connecticut and Rhode Island. Tour five (October to November) completed Lossing's northern travels in the Hudson Highlands near West Point.

In late November 1848, Lossing again left New York for sites in New Jersey and Pennsylvania (especially Philadelphia) that had been inconvenient during his earlier trips. He then headed south, touring from Maryland to Georgia for almost two months. In late January 1849, he left Charleston for New York, where he conducted more research, but mainly recorded his findings.[7] Meanwhile, Lossing initiated contacts with antiquarians throughout the United States (and a few in Canada) who supplied him with information or otherwise facilitated his progress.

Some of Lossing's earliest and most fruitful correspondence was with historians in New England.[8] Jared Sparks, biographer and editor then near his career's end, served as a major source for materials. Sparks also inspired Lossing to record his work's progress in a series of letters. One of his fullest statements on the *Field-Book*'s development appeared in a November 1849 note to Sparks. Here Lossing reported that so far "I have made a journey of nearly 8000 miles, and visited Every important locality[.]" Half of the approximately 600 engravings were ready, and the publishers were sticking to their plan of printing the book "on the finest paper and in the style of Harper's illustrated Bible, Shakespeare &c."

Further comments discussed the project's character and reception among antiquarians. "My plan is novel, and seems to commend itself to the good opinion of those who have examined the proof sheets. I combine the characteristics of a book of travel and of History, by giving a narrative of my journey to the places . . . and connecting therewith a record of the history appertaining to the locality. . . . It will be a sort of *topographical history*, if such a phrase may be allowed." While Lossing admitted the *Field-Book*'s "novel" aspects, he modestly refused to label his work's factual content as original. "I claim only to have been gleaning in the rich harvest field where yourself and others have reaped, and I propose to add my handful of gatherings to the sheaves of others."[9]

Lossing's work in the South brought him into contact with more antiquarians. In November 1848, Lossing left New York for his southern research trip. He visited Washington, D.C., where he used materials that historical editor Peter Force had collected. He also visited President James K. Polk, discussing with him the role Polk's ancestors played in the

Revolution. Lossing met George W. Parke Custis, George Washington's adopted step-son, whose memoirs Lossing later edited.[10]   From there, through December and early January 1849, Lossing moved south.

On January 6, near the Virginia-North Carolina border, Lossing paused to send his sister a letter on his impressions of the South. He apologized for not writing sooner, explaining that "I . . . have been as busy as a 'bee in a tar barrel' day and night, traveling on the road all day, and drawing and writing at night." He reported planters as "exceedingly kind," willing without fail to offer him a meal and quarters when he passed through their estates.   Although having already covered over 1,100 miles, Lossing recognized he still faced much travel.[11]

A week later, Lossing reached the Cowpens battlefield in northern South Carolina.   Pushing into the Palmetto State, Lossing noted low moral standards among slaves. "It is not often that they live together as man & wife over 4 or 5 years. . . . Owners are prohibited by law, [against] teaching their slaves to read or write. Though a great many of them are church members[,] scarcely any have any idea of what religion is, and many don't believe in a future state. . . . What a wretched condition! Are there not heathens here[?]"[12] Still, Lossing found southerners helpful regarding his research, making every possible effort to facilitate the good work.[13]

Lossing distanced himself from mercenary motives in his volumes' production. "It is not a work designed for merely winning dollars and cents, but . . . has in view the laudable purpose of foreseeing in a proper form, matters of general public interest connected with our Revolution."[14] Despite these sentiments' evident sincerity, Lossing still had to pay attention to practical publication issues. With the *Field-Book* such concerns grew paramount as the work expanded far beyond the size Lossing and his publishers had planned.

One document recorded the mixture of amazement and frustration that overtook Lossing and Harper & Brothers when they realized the project had attained unexpected proportions. According to the document, they originally planned a work of around 600 pages (only 40% of the final *Field-Book*'s length) that they estimated would cost $6,500 to produce. The final project cost over $11,200, with $9,500 of that going to Lossing and Barritt for the 1,100 engravings.[15] Contemporary reviews suggest Harpers and Lossing planned to first publish the *Field-Book* serially in twenty monthly "numbers," but it actually appeared in thirty installments. This probably decreased the project's profit margin, since subscribers to the entire series would have received more material for an initial fee.

Late 1852 found the second volume so near publication that many historians began congratulating Lossing on the great event. One remarked that "[h]owever pleasant the task of composing it may have been, yet there is a grateful sense of *relief* when it is once got through with." By mid-December, Lossing could inform friends that "[m]y Field[-]Book will be completed, and bound volumes on the publisher's shelves next week[.]" This prediction, unlike many others during the publication process, reached fulfillment just before Christmas, when Lossing told Jared Sparks that "[m]y 'Field Book' is now completed."[16] For both Lossing and Harpers, the publication task was over, but promotional activities began immediately.

A facet of these efforts grew apparent when Lossing wrote to several historians announcing Volume Two's completion. As he told North Carolina's David L. Swain, "[w]e are about to make application to the proper authorities to have the work placed in the School District Libraries of our State[.]"[17] These libraries, although serving schools and their pupils, also functioned as public libraries for local communities. In approaching the school district libraries and the state agencies that administered them, Harper & Brothers was continuing strategies they had used since the 1830s. This idea failed, but it did suggest Lossing's ingenuity and the lengths to which he went in publicizing the work.

Ingenuity was also evident within the *Field-Book*'s text, presenting a combination of solid historical research and engaging travelogue that contemporaries found attractive. The *Field-Book*'s most prominent stylistic feature was that Lossing narrated particular sites' histories not in the chronological order of relevant events, "as the mere historian would do"(I: 40n), but according to when he visited them. Thus Volume One began with a journal of Lossing's trip to upper New York and an analysis of the 1777 battle at Saratoga. Even within the first half of Volume One, this scheme created problems. After covering the Saratoga battle, for instance, Lossing discussed armies' movements in the days before that engagement. Similar confusion developed as Lossing covered U.S./Amerindian conflicts in Pennsylvania, and the French and Indian War (I: 131, 142, 173, 363).

Why did Lossing structure the *Field-Book* this way? Probably he wanted some device to distinguish his contribution from more conventional histories. He knew he worked in a well-plowed field, and this realization spurred him to create a unique work. Emphasis was on the Revolution not as its participants experienced it but on a more subjective level of Lossing's (and, vicariously, readers') discoveries and travels. Much of the *Field-Book*'s popularity sprang from the way its format helped Lossing bring the past more directly into the present.

Lossing's memoirs of his travels included many memorable descriptions of persons, places, hazards, and rewards he met, as when he offered a mock-heroic account of his adventures in sketching a pond on one battlefield. "I alighted in the rain, and made my way through tall wet grass and tangled vines, over a newly-cleared field, until I got a favorable view for the sketch here presented, which I hope the reader will highly prize, for it cost a pair of boots, a linen 'sack' ruined by the dark droppings from a cotton umbrella, and a box of cough lozenges" (I: 108).

The *Field-Book*'s interpretation offered a more detailed version of

Lossing's *Seventeen Hundred and Seventy-six*. In many ways, Lossing still depicted the Revolution as a contest between unsullied virtue and unredeemed evil, and he often oversimplified complexities of motivation within both Patriot and imperial camps. Lossing's own facetious description of the *Field-Book* summarized his perspective on its central themes: "The Pictorial/ Memorial/ Of the heart-trying time/ When with efforts sublime,/ Our patriot fathers cut Britain[']s proud thong[.]"[18]

Once in each volume, Lossing waxed eloquent over the Revolution as culminating America's "heroic" or "mythic" age. He linked the nation's founding with a general "crucible of progress," in which the colonial era played a vital role. This period, in turn, "ended when the work of the Revolution . . . was accomplished; when the bond of vassalage to Great Britain was severed by her colonies, and when the thirteen confederated States ratified a federal Constitution, and upon it laid the broad foundation of our Republic" (I: [xv]). A more veiled reference to a necessary national mythology appeared when Lossing narrated the heroism of a frontier woman in repulsing an Indian attack. Her achievement, he remarked, "ought to be perpetuated in marble, and preserved in the Valhalla of our Revolutionary heroes" (II: 292n).

Presenting the Revolution in this mythic light posed a conceptual problem of which Lossing might or might not have been aware. If the War for Independence represented a time of larger-than-life heroes and heroines, as conventional interpretations held, might not one view events since the nation's founding as betraying a decline of patriotic fervor among both leaders and the common people? And might not that, in turn, render a belief in national progress untenable? Essayist Lorenzo Sabine confronted this problem in the *North American Review*. His solution was to argue that, despite the high character of Washington and others, evil and selfishness had afflicted American public life throughout the Revolution.[19]

Lossing never broached this issue explicitly, but sometimes his approach had much in common with Sabine's. He admitted that not all patriots acted at a high level of virtue, although happily most gave a good account of themselves. This allowed Lossing to retain both great respect for the nation's founders and a faith that progress remained operative in American political and social life. But in other passages, as we will see, his view was not so sanguine: America really had declined and a recapture of Revolutionary virtue represented Americans' only hope of reversing the slide into oblivion.

Relatively few passages offered moral judgments on American patriots and soldiers, either to condemn or applaud their character and actions. Many more references were to specific American commanders, with George Washington receiving a predictably large share of these comments. Once Lossing admitted that:

Washington was not a brilliant man. In the distinctive fields of oratory, military command, or civil government, he has had many superiors. His surpassing greatness consisted in the harmonious combination and solidity of all the powers of mind and body which constitute a MAN in highest perfection. It was this combination and solidity which made his career a brilliant one—it is the contemplation of his character from this point of view which makes the world bow with reverence before the amazing dignity of his name and deeds. (II: 635n)

Discussions of Washington's and others' careers highlighted Lossing's need to accept or reject popular tales or "traditions" about them. Lossing's most common approach was to doubt legendary stories even if, like Mason Weems's tales about Washington, they served a laudable moral aim. As he commented about stories of Jane McCrea, a Loyalist maiden whom Indians allegedly murdered, "[i]t seems a pity to spoil the *romance* of the matter, but truth always makes sad havoc with the frost-work of the imagination, and sternly demands the homage of the historian's pen" (I: 97).

Elsewhere Lossing tried to hold to this "stern" rule. He considered tales of General Israel Putnam's exploits unlikely because "cotemporary [sic] history" did not support them (I: 212). He corrected statements of himself and others with an appeal to "[d]ocumentary evidence, which is far more reliable than the best tradition" (I: 706n). A similar judgment appeared when Lossing wrote of one manuscript that "[i]t is full, yet concise, and being official, with the signatures of the three principal officers engaged in the affair, attached, it is perfectly reliable" (II: 435).

Repeatedly Lossing moved beyond ideas about historical knowledge to speculate on that knowledge's personal and social meanings. His central contention was that history should serve as an important buttress of true, virtuous patriotism.

The love of country, springing up from the rich soil of the domestic affections, is a feeling consistent and coextensive with social union itself. . . . An honest, justified pride elevates the spirit of the citizen of a land so favored; makes him a vigilant guardian of its rights and honor, and inspires him with a profound reverence for the men and deeds consecrated by the opinions of the just as the basis upon which its glory rests.[20]

The best means of imbibing these lessons was for citizens to grow familiar with locales rich in historical-patriotic "associations"; hence the *Field-Book*'s approach to historical study. This agenda was always present in the *Field-Book*, but grew explicit in some passages. For instance, Valley Forge, site of Washington's 1777-1778 encampment, suggested the grandeur of patriotic suffering. "There, in the midst of frost and snows, disease and destitution, Liberty erected her altar. . . . Toward its 'templed hills,' consecrated by the presence and sufferings of those who achieved our independence, we journeyed, filled with the pleasant emotions of a pilgrim approaching the place he most adores" (II: 125).

But few people seemed to care about these places or their lessons. That Americans neglected, abused, or ignored their Revolutionary heritage was a constant theme in the *Field-Book*. Lossing justified his project on the grounds that only rare individuals possessed more than a superficial knowledge of the Revolution. Almost nobody could relate their learning to specific places. Further, contemporary acquisitive society put no value on the past and would let all its remains disappear unless someone recorded them. "I knew," he remarked, "that the genius of our people was the reverse of antiquarian reverence for the things of the past; that the glowing future, all sunlight and eminence, absorbed their thoughts and energies, and few looked back to the twilight and dim valleys of the past through which they had journeyed" (I: [vii], viii).

Lossing grieved over how Americans neglected the Revolutionary generation, refusing to honor them while they lived and leaving their graves in disrepair after they died. He thought that the lack of a momument to Nathaniel Greene was "[t]o the dishonor of our country" (I: 700n). Even some of the existent monuments were unworthy of the patriot dead—such as the pitiful stone at Lexington, Massachusetts (I: 553).

More criticisms surfaced as Lossing described Americans' abuse of historic sites. He admonished the owner of one building that had served as Washington's headquarters for letting the structure rot; he punished that offender by giving his name (II: 215). Lossing harbored no sympathy for those who remodeled historic buildings for selfish gain. He attacked entrepreneurs who turned Carpenter's Hall into an auctioneer's warehouse. "What a desecration! Covering the facade of the very Temple of Freedom with the placards of groveling mammon!" (II: 58). If possible, Lossing grew angrier when "scoundrel[s]" and "Vandal[s]" carried off pieces of monuments and old forts. He worried that the ruins of Fort Ticonderoga would disappear completely because so many tourists were carting off its remains (I: 128). He castigated the destruction of British general James Wolfe's monument as "Vandalism under the specious guise of reverence for the great" (I: 189). Elsewhere he labeled devotees of such amusements "heartless knaves or brainless fools" (I: 148).

References to Americans' use of their heritage extended to Lossing's perspective on other historians who wrote about the War for Independence. Some writers gained praise for their books' accuracy and other laudable qualities. Brantz Mayer, a lawyer and antiquarian, received an appreciative citation for his work on the southern colonies' Amerindian wars.[21] Women writers, especially Mercy Warren and Elizabeth Ellet, gained favorable references (II: 17n, 35n, 447n, 511n). Joel T. Headley, a fellow New Yorker who Lossing perhaps saw as a rival, fared less well. In one passage, Lossing criticized Headley for "carelessly" misunderstanding geography (I: 137n). But the severest censures of Headley came as Lossing dealt with military aspects of the Revolution.

When Lossing wrote the *Field-Book*, Headley was near the height of his fame for writing lurid military histories and biographies. Working with publisher Charles Scribner on most of his books, Headley won particular fame for *Napoleon and His Marshals* (1846) and *Washington and His Generals* (1847), both in two volumes, which went through many editions. During the Mexican War, Headley's instant histories of that conflict and biographies of its generals increased his popularity among juvenile and adult readers. Some considered Headley a sensationalistic, sentimental clown; hence Edgar Allan Poe's characterization of him as "the Autocrat of all the Quacks."[22]

Reviewers in the religious press found Headley more alarming than amusing due to his glorification of bloodshed. As one noted of his books, "[i]nculcating a blind worship of the war-god, they advance the warrior before all others, bidding statesmen, poets, and philosophers, succumb before him; and they hail war as the grand medicamentum that is to cure all ills, alleviate all burdens, procure all reforms, remedy all distress. And so the veil is removed from before the hideous demon whose throne is built upon human skulls."[23] Meanwhile, Lossing tried to avoid such tendencies in his history.

The *Field-Book* occasionally disparaged war with remarks on recent conflicts' devastating impact, as when Lossing described a trip with soldiers who were returning from the Mexican War (I: 35). More often Lossing criticized other historians for dwelling upon details of massacres or other atrocities. One attack came against William L. Stone, who wrote a competent but, Lossing thought, lurid book on the Wyoming Valley. He grew concerned because Stone, "not content with recording . . . bloody act[s] . ., lauds [them] as . . . deed[s] worthy of the highest praise" (I: 248n).

For his part, Lossing promised not to dwell on such incidents. "Thus far I have avoided such recitals, and I shall do so through the whole work before me. Neither pen nor pencil shall intentionally contribute one thought for a panegyric on war or its abettors" (I: 248). A section on the Battle of Guilford Court House made the same point. "Horrible, indeed, were many of the events of that battle; the recital will do no good, and I will forbear" (II: 404n).

In other passages Lossing proved himself willing to record just such details. He often felt compelled to justify the practice. Again discussing the Wyoming Valley, he explained that he offered specifics about murders Tories committed "to exhibit the infernal character which the passions of men assume when influenced by the horrid teachings in the school of war" (I: 269n). Sometimes Lossing's abhorrence for war expressed itself as simple outrage over its pointless slaughter and destruction. Even wars among Amerindians excited his horrified wonder, especially if they reminded him of whites' conflicts. "How many wars between Christian nations have originated in a quarrel about some miserable grasshopper!" (I: 343n).

Because war was such a scourge, Lossing had hope that humankind might eradicate it. "Henceforth our fortresses, and other paraphernalia of war, will have no other useful service to perform than to illustrate the history of a less enlightened age" (II: 325). But this sentiment did not restrain Lossing from occasionally finding sublime aspects in battle scenes. Of one navel engagement, Lossing remarked that "[t]he scene was one of appalling grandeur, while it exhibited men in the character of darkest furies" (II: 642). This was the irony of Lossing's perspective on warfare: he found it repulsive and fascinating at the same time.

Early reviewers of the *Field-Book* were almost unanimous in stressing its virtues. The *Methodist Quarterly Review* considered it especially appropriate reading as sectional tensions threatened American unity. "The remembrances of the Revolution are among the surest bonds of union, and the surest pledges of virtue, for the people of these States[;] and such a work as this, combining high art with pure patriotism and sound morality, deserves a wide diffusion among the people of every part of the land." Contentions that the *Field-Book* deserved wide sales merged with predictions of this result as reviewers lauded "this cheap though beautiful work[.]" *Godey's Ladies' Book* stated flatly that "[t]he work must be popular," and remarked that all American youths should peruse it.[24]

Not all notices had a favorable tone. Clergyman William Cruickshank wrote a diatribe against the *Field-Book* in the *American Whig Review*. He objected to Lossing's "maudlin sentimentality" and propensity for "turgid commonplace and asinine platitude," his "childish fondness for certain words and phrases" and "turgid and affected language[.]" At one point Cruickshank granted that Lossing's "merits" as a historian "are striking and original," but then noted errors in the *Field-Book*.[25]

Lossing's correspondence on the *Field-Book* was voluminous and continued at a heavy pace during the 1850s. Notes from historians and other writers accounted for much of this bulk. The comments Lossing and Harper & Brothers judged most laudatory served as raw material for promotional circulars that gave quotations from George Bancroft, Jared Sparks, Washington Irving, Edward Everett, and others.[26]

Many readers of the *Field-Book* contacted Lossing to speculate on why his work was good. Some readers enthused over the ways Lossing's celebration of both northern and southern heroism could lay foundations for sectional reconciliation. "[Y]ou have collected . . . many, [sic] interesting Relicks of our Revolution, embelished them with such beautiful illustrations and thrown around them the most instructive narrative," wrote a South Carolinian. Another antiquarian praised Lossing for his "unwearied pains in procuring facts; the care and accuracy in which these facts are presented, [which] must render it a *text book* for the *students* of our History."[27]

Some readers stressed the *Field-Book*'s travelogue aspect as a virtue. One correspondent told Lossing that "I like its *vagabondage* (meaning no disrespect to its author, but referring to its plan)." John A. McAllister, a Philadelphia antiquarian, confided that he habitually took Lossing's work while on trips to heighten his appreciation of places he visited. Another reader considered Lossing's merging of historical and travel literature crucial to "your interesting work . . . which you have dressed up in such novel attire as to make an old story new."[28]

Often readers commented less on specifics and more on the *Field-Book*'s likely impact on American culture. Several thought the work had already enshrined the forty-year-old Lossing among the immortals of national letters. As one noted, "[y]our countrymen will to the end of time be indebted to you for placing in their hands a book so patriotic & useful." Another predicted that the *Field-Book*'s fullest impact would grow evident as it inspired other historians. "Your volumes will do more towards the sale of all good books on the *great event* than all that have ever been written[.]"[29]

Lossing's correspondents who possessed specialized knowledge corrected mistakes in the *Field-Book*.[30] The most serious criticism along these lines came in May 1854, when Leonidas Polk, a Louisiana Episcopal bishop and later a Confederate general, objected to some statements about his grandfather in the *Field-Book*. Lossing, he charged, implied that Colonel Thomas Polk was among the North Carolina residents who accepted protection from Cornwallis—in other words, practically turned Tory. "As a descendant of the individual here mentioned, you will, I presume, recognize my right to ask you to furnish me the evidence" for the assertion, Polk demanded. Responding three weeks afterward, Lossing admitted that "I have already received letters from North Carolina, . . . in which are ample proofs that the inference . . . is not warranted by the real facts[.]" He then thanked Polk for his critique.[31] The *Field-Book*'s next edition contained no hint of the accusations.

Despite such incidents, the overwhelming majority of readers reacted positively to the *Field-Book*. Lossing's publishers were also pleased with the work, despite problems that developed after the first edition appeared. Most significantly, a fire in December 1853, destroyed their New York headquarters and burned all the unsold copies of the *Field-Book*'s first edition, although the stereotype plates and engravings survived.[32] One document, from around 1858, recorded the fire-loss at 6,000 copies out of the 16,000 Harpers had printed.[33] Undaunted, Harpers quickly rebuilt their establishment and began planning new editions of Lossing's work. In 1855 and 1859-1860, these plans reached fulfillment as they published two new editions. Precise sales figures for nineteenth-century American imprints are notoriously elusive, but the *Field-Book* was sufficiently important that some data have survived. In May 1855, for example, the publishers recorded a sale total to that date of 11,431 "numbers," 1,541 complete copies of Volume One and 1,990 of Volume Two.[34] In June 1856, a year after the

Field-Book's second edition appeared, Lossing sold his interest in the work to Harpers for just over $14,300.[35] But in terms of reputation, Lossing always had strong connections with the *Field-Book*, since this work set the pattern for his more successful books.

In the aftermath of the *Field-Book*, as Lossing tried to approach history through more conventional avenues (especially biography), he experienced both success and failure. Many of the projects he planned during this time either met with public apathy or never even led to actual publication. Eager to overcome these new obstacles, Lossing grew determined to find some project that might replicate the *Field-Book*'s novelty and popularity.

NOTES

1. H. T. Tuckerman, "William Beckford and the Literature of Travel," *Southern Literary Messenger* 16 (January 1850): 7-14; quotations on pp. 10-11.

2. "The Prize Question (No. 3) In Revolutionary Literature," *Publishers' Weekly* 9 (15 April 1876): 494. Here Lossing's work was the only one to appear on each of nineteen ballots. Lossing, *The Pictorial Field-Book of the Revolution,* 30 parts (New York: Harper and Brothers, 1850-52); revised edition 2 Vols. (New York: Harper and Brothers, 1855, 1860).

3. J. C. Derby, *Fifty Years Among Authors—Books and Publishers* [sic] (New York: G. W. Carleton & Co. [et. al.], 1884), p. 686.

4. Irving to Lossing, 4 January 1852, quoted in Ibid., p. 689.

5. Lossing quoted in Alexander Davidson, Jr., "How Benson J. Lossing Wrote His 'Field Books' of the Revolution, the War of 1812 and the Civil War," *The Papers of the Bibliographical Society of America* 32 (1938): 58. See also John T. Cunningham, "Historian on the Double," *American Heritage* 19 (June 1968): [54]-64, 78-81, especially 56-58.

6. Lossing to Warren C. Cram, 29 October 1888, Manuscript Division, New York State Library, Albany; Call No. BX 8951. One commentator asserted that Lossing devoted twenty months to the project, which would mean July 1848-April 1850. S. Austin Allibone, *A Critical Dictionary of English Literature and British and American Authors Living and Deceased.* 3 Vols. (Philadelphia: J. B. Lippincott & Co., 1882), I:1132. See also the references later in this chapter on the *Field-Book*'s publication process.

7. The preceding two paragraphs recount Lossing's record of his travels in the *Field-Book*.

8. Lossing to Longfellow, 21 October 1848; copy from Harvard University Library, MS Am 1340.2 (3538). Lossing to Longfellow 8 June 1850, Ibid. See also Lossing to Longfellow, undated [November 1850?], Ibid.

9. Lossing to Sparks, 12 November 1849, Sparks Manuscripts, Harvard University.

10. See especially Lossing's notebook from this trip, LS 1111, Lossing Collection, Huntington Library.

11. Lossing to Elizabeth Buck, 6 January 1849, Lossing Papers, Adriance Memorial Library, Poughkeepsie. A typescript of this letter appeared in a genealogical work at the same library: *The Buck Family of Dutchess County and Related Families*, comp.

Clifford M. Buck (n. p., 1963), pp. 81-85.

12. Lossing Notebook, LS 1111, Lossing Collection, Huntington Library.

13. An example was Thomas Smyth to Unidentified, 27 January 1849, LS 1834, Lossing Addenda Box 2, Ibid.

14. Lossing to John J. Smith, 23 December 1850, LS 210, Ibid.. Thanks are due Carolyn Sung of the Library of Congress for insights regarding this letter.

15. Undated [December 1852?] document, "The Pictorial Field Book of the Revolution," Lossing Addenda II, Box 33, Ibid..

16. Onderdonk to Lossing, 24 November 1852, Alexander Brown Papers, College of William & Mary, Box 3, Folder 56. Lossing to Swain, 18 December 1852, Swain Papers, Southern Historical Collection, University of North Carolina, Chapel Hill. Lossing to Sparks, 22 December 1852, Sparks Manuscripts, Harvard University.

17. Lossing to Swain, 18 December 1852 and 24 January 1853, Swain Papers, Southern Historical Collection, University of North Carolina, Chapel Hill. Lossing made the same statement in a 22 December 1852 letter to Jared Sparks, Sparks Manuscripts, Harvard University, and two 27 December 1852 letters, one to Henry W. Longfellow (Call. No. MS Am 1340.2 [3538], Harvard University), the other to George Bancroft (Bancroft Papers, Massachusetts Historical Society, Boston).

18. Lossing to Gen. Morris, 14 July 1857, New York State Library, Call No. 5422.

19. [Sabine], "The Past and the Present of the American People," *North American Review* 66 (April 1848): 426-46.

20. Volume I: [33]. In this connection, Lossing would have agreed with another writer: "[t]he scenes and occurrences of American independence are destined to form for succeeding ages a theme of inexhaustible and still-deepening interest—an interest more profound and earnest than we who live near the period are capable of estimating." "Historical Societies," *Home Journal*, 26 August 1848, p. 2 col. 3-4; quotation from col. 3.

21. Volume II: 283n. Bernard C. Steiner, "Brantz Mayer," *Maryland Historical Magazine* 5 (March 1910): 1-22.

22. Joel T. Headley, *Napoleon and His Marshals*, 2 Vols. (New York: Baker & Scribner, 1846); *Washington and His Generals*, 2 Vols. (New York: Baker & Scribner, 1847). For Poe's perspective, see the posthumous "Poe on Headley and Channing," *Southern Literary Messenger* 16 (October 1850): 610. Sources on Headley included: Evert A. Duyckinck and George L. Duyckinck, *Cyclopaedia of American Literature*. 2 Vols. (New York: Charles Scribner, 1856) II: 603-5; S. Austin Allibone, *A Critical Dictionary of English Literature and British and American Authors Living and Deceased*. 3 Vols. (Philadelphia: J.B. Lippincott & Co., 1882), I: 812-813; *History of Orange County, New York*, comp. E[dward] M. Ruttenber and L. H. Clark (Philadelphia: Everts & Peck, 1881), p. 360; *Portrait and Biographical Record of Orange County New York* (New York and Chicago: Chapman Publishing Co., 1895), pp. 139-40. See also Carl Bode, *The Anatomy of American Popular Culture 1840-1861* (Berkeley and Los Angeles: University of California Press, 1959), pp. 246-49; Owen Connelly and Jesse Scott, "Joel T. Headley," in *American Historians, 1607-1865*, ed. Clyde N. Wilson, Vol. 30 of *Dictionary of Literary Biography* (Detroit: Gale Research Company, 1984), pp. 107-11; Robert W. Johannesen, *To the Halls of the Montezumas: The Mexican War in the American Imagination* (New York and Oxford: Oxford University Press, 1985).

23. "D.," "Headley's Histories," *Methodist Quarterly Review* 30 [3rd ser 8] (January 1848): 84-103; quotations on pp. 86, 101. See also "Washington and His Generals," *The American Review: A Whig Journal* 5 (May 1847): 517-34; "Headley's Washington and His Generals, Volume II.," *The American Review* (June 1847): 638-42; "Headley's Writings," *New Englander* 5 (July 1847): 402-15; "Martial Men and Martial Books," *New Englander* 6 (October 1848): 482-98. A more positive assessment appeared in "Bookstore Chat," *Home Journal*, 8 May 1847, p. 3 col. 1.

24. "Short Reviews and Notices of Books," *Methodist Quarterly Review* 32 [4th Series 2] (July 1850): 484. See also *The* [Burlington, Vermont] *Daily Free Press*, 26 October 1850, p. 2 col. 2-3; "Literary Notices," *Home Journal*, 15 June 1850, p. 3 col. 1. Other significant reviews appeared in that column on the following dates: 25 May 1850, p. 3 col. 2; 6 July 1850, p. 3 col. 1; 31 August 1850, p. 2 col. 4; 22 February 1851, p. 4 col. 1; 22 March 1851, p. 3 col. 1; 30 August 1851, p. 3 col. 3. "Editors' Book Table," *Godey's* 41 (September 1850): 185; *Godey's* (November 1850): 314. See also the same column for December 1850, p. 381; and, among many others, "Editor's Table," *The Knickerbocker* 36 (July 1850): 107; "Literary Notices," *The New Englander* 8 (November 1850): 654-55.

25. "Lossing's Field Book of the Revolution," *The American Whig Review* n. s. 10, [whole 16] (September 1852): 225-44; quotations from pp. 229-30, 231, 233, 236, 237.

26. Different versions of these circulars were in the Lossing Collection, Hayes Library, Box 20.

27. Charles Phillips to Lossing, 24 November 1851, Mecklenburg Declaration Papers, Southern Historical Collection, University of North Carolina, Chapel Hill; William Hazzard to Lossing, 10 January 1852, typescript of original in War of 1812 Collection, Volume 5, Clements Library, University of Michigan; J. Wheeler to Lossing, 28 June 1852, Lossing Collection, Syracuse University Library, Box 1. See also R. A. Sommerville to Lossing, 18 April 1857, Lossing Collection, Ibid..

28. J. [?] Callaghan to Lossing, Mid-January [sic] 1852, Lossing Collection, Hayes Library, Box 3; McAllister to Lossing, 5 June 1857, Lossing Collection, Historical Society of Pennsylvania; W. W. Hazard to Lossing, 28 May 1854, Alexander Brown Papers, College of William and Mary Library, Box 3, folder 53.

29. Ebenezer Griffin to Lossing, 5 March 1853, LS 736, Lossing Addenda Box 3, Lossing Collection, Huntington Library. Baird to Lossing, 4 April 1853, LS 338, Ibid.

30. D. S. Broadman to Lossing, on following dates: 16 September 1850, 15 January 1851, 3 May 1851, 3 July 1851, 21 January 1852, 26 April 1852, 12 July 1852, 3 September 1852, 3 February 1853, all in the Autograph File, Harvard University. On Swain's corrections, see especially two Lossing to Swain letters, 23 September 1852 and 23 May 1853, both in the Swain Papers, Southern Historical Collection, University of North Carolina, Chapel Hill, and E. W. Carutters to Swain, 21 March 1856, Swain Papers, Ibid.. Among many other examples, these were most illuminating: Darlington to Lossing, 22 September 1854, LS 548, Lossing Addenda Box 3, Lossing Collection, Huntington Library; S. E. Potter to Lossing, 29 January 1855, Lossing Collection, Syracuse University Library, Box 1; J. H. Tyng to Lossing, n.d. [ca. 1853?], Lossing Collection, Hayes Library, Box 8.

31. Polk to Lossing, 20 May 1854, Polk Papers, Library of Congress. I first read this letter on a microfilm of that collection in the Southern Historical Collection, University of North Carolina, Chapel Hill. William M. Polk reprinted this letter and related manuscripts in *Leonidas Polk: Bishop and General*. 2 Vols. (New York:

Longmans, Green, and Co., 1894), I: 19. The controversial passage appeared in the *Field-Book*'s first edition, 2 Vols. (New York: Harper and Brothers, 1850-52) I: 625. Lossing to Polk, 12 June 1854, same collections. This letter also appeared in Polk, *Leonidas Polk*, I, pp. 20-21 and in the Lyman C. Draper Papers, Series GG: Mecklenburg Declaration Papers, Vol. 1, pp. 57-58, State Historical Society of Wisconsin.

32. One friend felt relief over the illustrations' survival, calling it "a great mercy & a great blessing." Francis Virtue to Lossing, 20 December 1853, Lossing Collection, Syracuse University Library, Box 1.

33. Undated [ca. 1858?] Memo, Lossing Addenda Box 28, Lossing Collection, Huntington Library.

34. Undated [ca. 1855?] Statement of Harper & Brothers Account, Lossing Collection, Syracuse University Library, Box 3.

35. The exact figure was $14,303.76. "Assignment to Harper & Brothers . . . ," 17 June 1856, Harpers Archives, Reel 1, Contract Books, Vol. 1, p. 278; see also Reel 53, Correspondence Relating to Contracts, Box 18.

6

WORTH A DOZEN PLUTARCHS: THE 1850s

To recall the *Southern Literary Messenger*'s categories from Chapter 1, nineteenth-century American writers often moved quickly between scholarly attainment and "scribbler" status. This was true for Lossing, who, through the 1850s, sought to further his career through many projects. A focus for this period was in biography, which Lossing viewed as a source for history's moral teachings. Some of his biographical works from these years proved memorable for contemporary readers. *Our Countrymen*, a volume of brief articles on significant Americans, impressed one antiquarian as "worth a dozen Plutarchs" in its potential for instructing youth.[1] Other biographical productions met with less praise. A work on Daniel Boone did not even reach print. But in all his books of the period, Lossing worked from fairly consistent intellectual and commercial aims.

Two such themes require particular comment. First, a concern to exploit biography for life examples appeared in most of Lossing's works in these years, but especially the volume of collective biography, *Our Countrymen*. Among other reasons, this held significance for expressing assumptions about what would most likely encourage readers to buy his books.

Second, Lossing's works of the 1850s deepened his concern to offer interpretations that would inspire as little controversy as possible. This trend partly reflected marketing strategy, but also sprang from his desire for national unity as necessary to fulfill the nation's potential. Lossing did not ignore political or social conflict, but he often depicted such problems as exceptional in the national experience and not worth extended treatment. When dissent from his viewpoints appeared among reviewers, usually due to sectional tensions, Lossing characterized their arguments as dangerous to a consensus he desperately wanted to forge.

Completion of the *Field-Book of the Revolution* brought Lossing fame and a high standing among antiquarians, general readers, and publishers. But the years that followed the great work's appearance were not ones of ease or even moderated labor for him. Indeed, in the 1850s Lossing entered a dizzying round of writing and related activities that sometimes bore fruit but in other instances repaid him only with frustration. By 1860 Lossing was still trying to recapture the *Field-Book*'s success. Meanwhile, he worked hard to cultivate ties with several publishers, with links to Harper & Brothers among the most significant.

In June 1850, Harper & Brothers initiated *Harper's New Monthly Magazine*. Quickly that periodical became a force in national letters; the first issue's circulation of 7,500 reached 50,000 by year's end. On the negative side, some commentators attacked it for devoting too much space to English and other foreign writers.[2] The charge contained much truth, although *Harper's* also published many indigenous essays and book excerpts. The editors also displayed a willingness to inform readers on various fields of applied and theoretical intellectual endeavor, as when they discoursed on history's nature and utility.[3] These discussions were neither original nor profound, but they helped readers to develop a framework for the magazine's historical essays, many of which Lossing wrote.

Lossing supplied engravings for *Harper's* from the first issue, and soon his historical reputation stimulated the editors to solicit essays from him. In 1850 and 1851, Lossing's contributions exploited his Revolutionary research for topics and interpretations.[4] One paper did broach a distinct topic: the recent experiences of American explorers in the Arctic. Lossing applauded cooperative Anglo-American efforts to find missing British sailors, an endeavor he perceived as a harbinger of future peaceful relations between the two powers, and perhaps among all nations.[5]

Soon Lossing's essays began to encompass a wide range of topics. Deviant American religious groups gained his attention in two articles. A paper on "The Mormons" presented a brief history of the sect and its emigration to the West. Lossing characterized Joseph Smith, the Mormon Prophet, as "an illiterate and not over-scrupulous young man," and repeatedly called his disciples "dupes." He labeled the Mormon practice of polygamy "monstrous," but did not justify the group's opponents who killed Smith and others. "This cruel persecution of thousands of innocent people, is a lasting stain upon the character not only of Missouri, but the boasted enlightened age in which we live."

Lossing granted of the Latter Day Saints that "this wonderful people" displayed "indomitable perseverance and surprising energy[.]" Later he reiterated this point, but also offered dire predictions of polygamy's impact. "The surface of society [in the Mormon state, Deseret] exhibits the aspect of the highest degree of public and private virtue and sound morality. But the poison is at work secretly; and not many years will elapse before its effects will be seen on the surface of the body politic."

Were the Mormons only destroying themselves, Lossing might have expressed minimal ill-ease. But he also worried, as contemporary nativists did about Catholicism, that Mormon values represented a threat to republican government. "What will be the result of the consolidation of such a people, one in interest and faith, in the heart of our continent, whose acknowledged head is supreme in all things, spiritual, temporal, social, and political, is a question worthy of the profound attention of statesmen and political economists."[6]

Less ominous was an essay on a Shaker colony that also offered a general perspective on that religious group.[7] This sect inspired interest and controversy throughout the nineteenth century, partly for their strict communal social organization and celibacy but also for their pacifism. The Shakers' high reputation for domestic crafts and manufacturing caused Americans to see their settlements as tourist attractions.[8] It was in this spirit that Lossing visited the Lebanon Valley, New York community in August 1856.

From the outset, Lossing seemed favorably disposed toward the Shakers, since the community's laudable neatness and industry were the first attributes that struck him. He attended a worship service, concluding that "there was nothing in the entire performance calculated to elicit any other than feelings of deepest respect and serious contemplation. . . . The music was unlike any thing [sic] I had ever heard; beautiful, impressive, and deeply solemn." Pages following described the community's system of domestic manufacture, which Lossing depicted favorably. "Having property in common, the people have no private ambitions nor personal cares; and being governed by the pure principles of their great leading doctrines, they seem perfectly contented and happy."

Lossing retained his respectful tone while outlining the sect's beliefs. He granted that, for him, marriage seemed a spiritually advantageous condition. But his admiration for the Shakers' honest advocacy of celibacy persisted. "I am convinced, from observation and from the testimony of their immediate neighbors, that they live in strict accordance with their professions. . . . Surely the sacrifices of the dearest interests of earth are sufficient guarantees of their sincerity. Call it all delusion if you will, the impregnable fact that they have maintained their integrity and their faith for seventy years is vastly significant." For any of various possible reasons, Lossing interpreted this celibate communion far more charitably than he had the Mormons. Rather than representing a threat to society's values, the Shakers confirmed such American values as industry and moral restraint.[9]

Meanwhile, Lossing had several other projects in process. One work was *Our Countrymen*, a compilation of over three hundred brief biographies of deceased Americans.[10] In writing this book, as with an earlier volume on the Declaration of Independence's signers, Lossing entered a field of literary endeavor already familiar to Americans. Earlier Jeremy Belknap, Jared

Sparks, and Samuel L. Knapp wrote or edited influential works in the genre.[11] Even as Lossing wrote *Our Countrymen*, several less distinguished writers composed works that typically emphasized military or political leaders.[12] Lossing's contribution covered that conventional ground, but also much more.

Lossing began contemplating a work of collective biography in 1854, planning to work on it while attending his wife, then ill at home. He soon reached an agreement with a New York firm, Ensign, Bridgman & Fanning, for its publication. The book appeared in the late spring of 1855 to almost universally positive reviews. One newspaper labeled it "a most welcome contribution to our popular literature." Another remarked that "Mr. Lossing is a public benefactor, for he ever studies to bring to the minds of his countrymen memorials of their country's heroes. . . . The important lessons of truth and fearlessness, of bravery and integrity, presented in this volume, will make this work exceedingly popular among the youth of our land." Several notices repeated that prediction of wide sales; unfortunately no record survived of whether this proved correct.[13]

Our Countrymen asserted Lossing's concern to make history a tool for American youth's moral uplift. History, in Lossing's view, always carried a moral component, but this grew particularly evident as he contemplated the lives of great men and women. In this book, concern with moral didacticism found expression in both familiar and unusual ways. Lossing was conventional in discussing the moral qualities of Revolutionary and other figures that deserved emulation or rejection. But other aspects of Lossing's essays on American worthies were unique, even disquieting for some readers.

Lossing's ideas on race surfaced in some controversial articles on Black women. His inclusion of essays on female slaves, such as the poet Phyllis Wheatley, led one North Carolina critic to censure *Our Countrymen*. That writer satirized Lossing's respect for Wheatley and Catherine Ferguson, a pious slave who had died not long before the book appeared.

Why, among this galaxy of great and good men, soldiers, artists[,] statesmen and divines, Mr. Lossing has thought proper to introduce two ladies of color, with comfortable-looking portraits of each appended, we are at some loss to determine. —Why should Aunt Phillis and Aunt Katy, [sic] be so gallantly handed down to posterity in company with Ames and Turledge, any more than any other unpretending and respectable females who teach Sabbath schools and indulge in writing marvellously bad doggrel, [sic] all over the land? We protest against such levelling of position and reputation.[14]

Responding to the criticism in a letter to antiquarian David Swain, Lossing expressed sadness over the reviewer's bigotry and the impact such views were having on America. "I am no abolitionist, as the term is used. Far from it. But, my friend, it is from such expressions of *prejudice* as these on one side, and the over-zealous ebullitions of *fanaticism* on the other, that all the sectional heart-burnings in our land, are born."[15]

Criticism also dogged Lossing's first book intended explicitly for school use: 1854's *Pictorial History of the United States*. Educational reform had concerned Lossing since his early years, so this delay in writing and marketing a school history may appear incongruous. Why had Lossing not entered this field earlier? In one sense he had, since several of his books from the late 1840s appealed especially to younger readers. But only from the 1850s onward did Lossing produce books that included examination questions and other classroom supplements. Contemporaries' awareness that schools should more carefully teach the nation's history may have stimulated Lossing to write these.[16] As in his many biographical projects from these years, his first schoolbook offerings revealed how Lossing vigorously exploited what he saw as growing markets for historical literature.

The original publisher for the *Pictorial History* was F. J. Huntington of New York, a magazine editor who dabbled in other projects.[17] Lossing had the manuscript ready early in 1854, but problems with the book's printing delayed it through that spring. When the book finally appeared, Lossing was able to take advantage of schools' needs for the new academic year. Just before Christmas, he told one friend that the first edition of 4,000 copies was nearly exhausted and that Huntington planned a second run of 6,000.[18]

Public reaction to the book gave Lossing further hope, although in this he also met setbacks. Lossing's personal correspondents were almost unanimous in acclaiming the *Pictorial History*.[19] More censorial was a notice in *The Independent*, a religious newspaper that counted Henry Ward Beecher and his sister, Harriet Beecher Stowe, among its editors. Its review began positively, lauding the book's illustrations and clearly written text. Then suddenly the notice made critical comments about what its writer judged as a lack of sufficiently harsh words for slavery. Specifically, *The Independent* thought Lossing should have criticized aspects of the 1850 Compromise that favored the South. "Mr. Lossing . . . is less fortunate in his narrative of recent events in which the great principles of human rights were . . . involved. . . . Parents and teachers who value truth in history, can not scrutinize too closely such partisan representations in school-books for the young."[20]

How justified was this critique? The *Pictorial History*'s references to the 1850 Compromise took up half of Lossing's brief section on Zachary Taylor's administration. Here he granted the seriousness of conditions before the agreement, noting that "never before did civil war appear so inevitable. Happily for the country," though, "some of the ablest statesmen and patriots the Republic had ever gloried in, were members of the national legislature, at that time, and with consummate skill they directed and controlled the storm." He praised Henry Clay, the agreement's originator, although admitting in a footnote that the Compromise's provisions for the capture and return of fugitive slaves "produced, and continues to produce, much dissatisfaction at the North; and the execution, evasion and violation of the law, in several instances, have led to serious disturbances and much bitter sectional feeling."[21]

These comments, purposefully vague on significant points but celebratory in their perspective on the nation's political leaders, revealed Lossing trying to admit sectional tensions' presence while assuming that Americans could solve such problems. Twenty years before, in some unpublished poetry, he lauded America's greatness and expressed assurance that no political conflict could hinder its destiny of spreading justice and equity throughout the world. Now, in a medium he saw as especially suited to a rising generation, Lossing gave detailed attention to political "disturbances." Whether consciously or not, his final comments could have hinted that he blamed Abolitionists for these problems. Between this book and *Our Countrymen*, ironically enough, Lossing had tried to soothe sectional tensions but only succeeded in drawing criticism from both sides.

Lossing's response to the *Independent*'s attack came in another letter to David Swain, who concurred in rejecting the "rabid" criticism. Lossing could scarcely contain his contempt at what he considered a demeaning attack from those whose views might prove dangerous to the nation. "Such things are, to me, exceedingly disgusting. If our Union is ever *destroyed*, it will be the work of *fanatics* of the North and the South," including Beecher and Mrs. Stowe.[22]

Meanwhile other projects piqued public interest, although not always as Lossing planned or expected. Lossing devoted attention to publicizing and preserving Washington's estate at Mount Vernon, Virginia. Through the 1850s, many journalists, orators, and antiquarians noted the urgency of saving Washington's mansion and gravesite, then allegedly suffering neglect in his descendants' hands.[23] From 1853, the South Carolina native Ann Pamela Cunningham labored through the Mount Vernon Ladies' Association of the Union to buy the estate and led Edward Everett and others to work in the project's auspices.[24] Even while planning and editing other books, Lossing had a role in these efforts.

The most detailed description of Washington's estate and its relics appeared in Lossing's volume, *Mount Vernon and Its Association*.[25] He wrote this book quickly after an early 1859 visit during which he met Miss Cunningham of the Association. *Mount Vernon* appeared early that summer and received effusive praise from Cunningham, her coworkers and other readers. But a depressed book trade limited sales, especially outside New York. As an agent in Philadelphia reported, "Mount Vernon is very well received here—the only hindrance [sic] to the sale of it being the hardness of the times. The screws have been a turn or two more in this city than in yours."[26]

Some of Lossing's works did not find sufficient encouragement to reach print. Despite their abortive character, such activities were important for establishing a context for changes in Lossing's research agenda, especially his efforts to recapture *The Field-Book of the Revolution*'s success through a work on the War of 1812.

The failed project to which Lossing devoted the most energy was a biography of Daniel Boone that he and Lyman C. Draper planned as a collaborative effort. This would, they hoped, initiate a series of similar works on other pioneer figures. This effort, which lasted six years until both parties recognized they would never write the books, was Lossing's most frustrating excursion into historical research. More than anything else, it convinced him that he should de-emphasize biography and concentrate on the pictorial works upon which his fame rested.

As with Washington, Boone's life occasionally found a place in Lossing's earlier books. *The Field-Book of the Revolution* contained a long biographical sketch that revealed Lossing already knew much about Boone. *Our Countrymen* included an essay on the pioneer in which Lossing noted that Boone's mythic stature "partakes so largely of the spirit of chivalry and true romance, that we . . . look upon him with a sentiment of hero-worship."[27] Meanwhile Draper, a Buffalo, New York, native who moved to Wisconsin in 1853, was assembling a voluminous collection of manuscripts about Boone and other western heroes in the fledgling State Historical Society of Wisconsin. He also dreamed of literary conquests that might arise from his work.[28]

The endeavor began in March 1854, when Draper's Society elected Lossing to its ranks. Lossing thanked Draper for the honor and asked about using his manuscripts. In response, Draper proposed the biography series and asked Lossing to relocate to Wisconsin to facilitate the work. Lossing declined to move, but did visit Draper that summer. They agreed to divide work and expenses equally, with Draper arranging primary materials and Lossing editing them into narrative form. Work proceeded into 1855, although an injury to Draper's writing hand slowed progress. Finally Lossing suggested that Draper simply arrange materials chronologically and send them to him.[29]

The project aroused considerable interest among antiquarians and periodical editors. In choosing to begin their series with Boone, Draper and Lossing selected a topic that interested many other writers; yet the field was not overburdened with published works.[30] Periodical references to the Lossing-Draper partnership began appearing in May 1854; several more reached print that autumn. Publicity stimulated impatience among antiquarians, as when one remarked in 1855 that "I suppose, we shall now have some of those Draper Books under way—Pray when may we expect Danl. Boone?" Anticipation persisted in 1857, when Francis Parkman remarked to Draper that "I was glad to see by yr. circular that your league with Mr. Lossing still continues & will soon issue in the publication of some of yr. treasures—but don't make the book merely *popular*."[31]

With others' expectations to encourage Draper and Lossing, why did the Boone project fail to produce anything substantive?[32] One problem was that they had trouble selecting a publisher. Even before the financial panic of 1857 the book trade was not healthy, and Draper and Lossing had to expend much effort to make favorable arrangements. In 1854, they nearly committed to Harper & Brothers, although even Lossing was not certain this would prove wise. "Perhaps we may do better, than with Harpers, although I doubt." In 1859, Lippincott's of Philadelphia seemed to hold the inside track,[33] although by that time other forces had pushed the project almost totally from the pair's minds.

For Draper, a variety of work-related, health, and personality factors converged to render Boone's biography impractical. Most important, Draper had a constitutional inability to write while a possibility existed that unknown documents might surface. This conviction that anything he wrote had to be definitive nearly paralyzed Draper and played a role in his writing only one book.[34]

In Lossing's case, the most serious personal setback came in 1854 as his wife Alice developed uterine cancer. She rallied a few times but, by October, Lossing admitted that "I somewhat fear that my dear wife's difficulty may prove more serious than I had hoped." Indeed Alice's condition was serious; after months of illness she finally died on April 18, 1855. Lossing felt intense grief which damaged his health; as a result he visited several spas that summer, further delaying the work with Draper.[35]

Lossing's life remained unsettled for over a year while he courted and married Helen Sweet, the daughter of a prosperous farmer. In late 1855, he began visits with her family; Helen's diary recorded some of his conversations, so his presence was noteworthy for her. Thomas Sweet, Helen's father, died in September 1856; Lossing's support through this time drew the couple even closer together. On November 15, 1856, the local Episcopal Rector married them.

Their relationship, throughout the rest of Lossing's life but especially in these years, reflected much heartfelt affection. As Lossing wrote in 1857, "[m]ore and more we become *one*." In May 1858, the Lossings had their first child—a boy, whom Lossing named after John, his father. Three weeks later Lossing recorded his joy with his wife in a journal. "At the present I am extremely happy. She is all that I can desire, and in giving me a child she has brought me a blessing for which I had lost all hope."[36] For the first decade of their marriage, the Lossings lived in New York City, although they made frequent trips to the Sweet's homestead near Poughkeepsie, which Helen had inherited. Lossing quickly developed an attachment to the rural home and left the city to visit it whenever possible. "I have a delightful home here above the Highlands, in the midst of a rich cultivated country on the banks of the Hudson," he wrote in 1858. After the Civil War this farm, which Lossing renamed "the Ridge," became their home.[37]

But the major factor working against a partnership with Draper was professional, not personal. Throughout the 1850s, Lossing conducted research on a project he hoped would recapture *The Field-Book of the Revolution*'s success: a pictorial history of the second war with England. Even as his association with Draper began, this project remained a high priority.[38] By decade's end, that project so riveted Lossing's attention that work on Boone seemed a needless distraction.

As early as 1851 Lossing contemplated a history of the Second Anglo-American War along the *Field-Book* model.[39] Writing to antiquarians, he revealed that he hoped to include a narrative of developments even before 1812, and they responded favorably.[40] In 1853, publication rights for the work became an issue. Early that year, while conducting research in Washington, D.C., Lossing met the publisher J. B. Lippincott who, Lossing claimed, coveted the work "for he is sure it will have an immense sale." Yet just a few days later, Lossing seemed to assume that Harper & Brothers would handle it. Still, Lossing objected to *Harper's* plan for printing Joel T. Headley's articles on the war as "presenting serious interference with our Enterprise." Not until 1859 was the firm's control of the project certain.[41]

In 1860, with contract in hand, Lossing proceeded to make research on the War of 1812 his central task. He developed a circular for persons with relevant manuscript materials or personal recollections,[42] and planned research trips, particularly to the Midwest and South. In January, he announced to one friend "that I am preparing to go out upon the war-path in the early Summer." Actually August began before Lossing started his journey through Western New York and the Niagara frontier. In September and early October, Lossing visited Ohio and Indiana,[43] after which he began planning a southern tour.

Heightened sectional tensions surrounding the presidential election of 1860 caused emotional conflict about visiting the South. In early November, on election eve, Lossing planned to make the trip, prompting one friend to ask when he expected to return.[44] In December, after South Carolina's secession, contacts there hinted that Lossing might be wise to change his plans. Novelist and essayist William G. Simms affirmed his interest in Lossing's project and his willingness to lend aid, but added: "[P]ermit me to counsel you to forbear your visit at the present juncture." Simms thought that Lossing's inquiries about local fortifications would raise suspicions that he was a spy. "Even were there no danger, you would hardly find any citizen prepared to give his attention to researches touching a war of 50 years ago, while he is preparing for one" that could begin at any time.[45]

Notwithstanding this warning, Lossing decided to proceed with his trip. In Washington, D.C., just before Christmas, he wrote to his wife that he would return home soon, perhaps by January 1, 1861.[46] But then he started west instead: into Virginia and Tennessee, and finally to New

Orleans.

He was still in Louisiana in April 1861, when the Confederate attack on Fort Sumter culminated sectional tensions and thrust Lossing into a new war and a new vision of history. His concern regarding interpretations that all Americans could accept became less evident. Even when Lossing proposed unified visions of the national past, as sometimes happened in the 1860s and later, specifics of his viewpoint proved far different than had been the case before the Civil War revised his perspective on America's past, present, and future.

NOTES

1. John W. Francis to Lossing, 25 May 1855, Lossing Collection, Syracuse University Library, Box 1.

2. A good example was: AN AMERICAN WRITER [sic], "A Letter to the Proprietors of Harpers' Magazine," *The American Whig Review* n. s. 10, [whole 16] (July 1852): 12-20. On the magazine's history and Lossing's and other historical writers' parts in it, see Frank Luther Mott, *A History of American Magazines 1850-1865* (Cambridge, Mass.: Harvard University Press, 1938), especially pp. 386-93. The circulation figures came from a March 1888 column reprinted in *Harper's Lost Reviews*, comp. Clayton L. Eichelberger (Millwood, N.Y.: KTO Press, 1976), p. 107.

3. "Editor's Table. History is Philosophy Teaching by Example," *Harper's* 4 (April 1852): 700-2.

4. Through this time, Lossing contributed three signed essays on the Revolution that served as lead articles: "A Pilgrimage to the Cradle of American Liberty. With Pen and Pencil," *Harper's* 1 (November 1850): [721]-29; "Our National Anniversary," *Harper's* 3 (July 1851): [145]-60; "The Boston Tea Party," *Harper's* 4 (December 1851): [1]-11. He signed another paper but it was not a lead essay: "The Treason of Benedict Arnold," *Harper's* 3 (September 1851): 451-60. For a positive comment on this article, see "Literary Notices," *Home Journal* 6 September 1851, p. 3 col. 3.

5. "The American Arctic Expedition," Harper's 4 (December 1851): 11-22. This unsigned article followed immediately Lossing's signed "Boston Tea Party" piece.

6. "The Mormons," *Harper's* 6 (April 1853): 605-22. Quotations, in order, from pp. 605, 607, 608, 613, 621, 612, 605, 621, 619, 621, 622. Another magazine essay on the Mormons was a similar compound of disdain and admiration; but its anonymous writer, unlike Lossing, did not consider the Saints a threat to American institutions. "Nauvoo and Deseret," *The National Magazine* 4 (June 1854): [481]-89.

7. "The Shakers," *Harper's* 15 (July 1857): 164-77. One New York literary magazine gave particular attention to this essay, remarking on how the latest *Harper's* included a "capital account of the Shakers, with some very graphic illustrations, both of which we take to be the work of that favorite surveyor of knowledge for the people—Benson J. Lossing." "Knick," "Literary Intelligence," *American Publishers' Circular and Literary Gazette* 3 (11 July 1857): 437.

Don Gifford edited this article and reproduced many of Lossing's original sketches for its illustrations in *An Early View of the Shakers: Benson John Lossing and the Harper's Article of July 1857* (Hanover and London: University Press of New England for Hancock Shaker Village, Inc., 1989). Gifford assembled much useful information in this slender book, but the citations that follow are from the original article. Reproductions of some of Lossing's sketches appeared in "An Artist Among the Shakers," *American Heritage* 31 (April/May 1980): 69-73. Robert P. Emlen discussed Lossing's work in *Shaker Village Views: Illustrated Maps and Landscape Drawings by Shaker Artists of the Nineteenth Century* (Hanover and London: University Press of New England, 1987), pp. 186-87.

8. On the second theme, see "Memorial of the People Called Shakers," *The Friend of Peace* 3 (1824): 284-86. Among twentieth-century discussions, see Edward Deming Andrews, *The People Called Shakers: A Search for the Perfect Society* (New York: Oxford University Press, 1953); Henri Desroche, *The American Shakers: From Neo-Christianity to Presocialism*, trans. and ed. John K. Savacool (Amherst, Mass.: University of Massachusetts Press, 1971); Flo Morse, *The Shakers and the World's People* (New York: Dodd, Mead & Co., 1980); Lawrence Foster, *Religion and Sexuality: The Shakers, the Mormons and the Oneida Community* (Champaign, Ill.: University of Illinois Press, 1984); June Sprigg and David Larkin, *Shaker: Life, Work, and Art* (New York: Stewart, Tabori & Chang, 1987). On the tourist aspect, see June Sprigg, "Out of This World," *American Heritage* 31 (April/May 1980): 65-68.

9. "The Shakers," pp. 168, 168-69, 175, 177. Nearly twenty years later, a less elaborate anonymous article made comments similar to Lossing's. "The Shakers in Niskayuna," *Frank Leslie's Popular Monthly* 20 (December 1875): 663-70 and 672.

10. Lossing, *Our Countrymen; or, Brief Memoirs of Eminent Americans* (New York: Ensign, Bridgman & Fanning; Philadelphia: Lippincott, Grambo & Co., 1855).

11. Jeremy Belknap, *American Biography.* Vol. I (Boston: Isaiah Thomas & E. T. Andrews, 1794); Vol. II (Boston: Isaiah Thomas & E. Andrews, 1798). *The Library of American Biography*, ed. Jared Sparks, First Series, 10 Vols. (Boston: Hilliard, Gray, 1834-1838) and later series. Harper and Brothers later held rights to the Library. See "Sparks' American Biography," *Methodist Quarterly Review* 30 [3rd ser 8] (October 1848): 505-14. Samuel L. Knapp, *American Biography* (New York: Conner & Cooke, 1833) and later editions; on that work and Knapp in general, see Ben Harris McClary, "Samuel Lorenzo Knapp and Early American Biography," *Proceedings of the American Antiquarian Society* 95 (1) (1985): 39-67. For a through discussion of this genre, see Gordon M. Marshall, "The Golden Age of Illustrated Biographies: Three Case Studies," in *American Portrait Prints: Proceedings of the Tenth Annual American Print Conference*, ed. Wendy Wick Reaves (Charlottesville, Va.: University Press of Virginia for the National Portrait Gallery[,] Smithsonian Institution, 1984), pp. 29-82.

12. For example, *Daring Deeds of American Heroes with Biographical Sketches*, ed. James O. Brayman (New York and Auburn, N.Y.: Miller, Orton & Mulligan, 1856).

13. Lossing discussed his plans in a letter to H. Phelps, 10 November 1854, Lossing Collection, Hayes Library, Box 1. The publishers issued *Our Countrymen* in late May 1855, in a 12 mo. edition that cost $1.50 per copy. "New Works—American, English and French," *Norton's Literary Gazette and Publishers' Circular* 2 (1 June 1855): 241. Meanwhile, in Philadelphia, Lippincott, Grambo & Co. did a first run of 3,000. Lossing to Lyman C. Draper, 23 May 1855, Draper Correspondence, State Historical Society of Wisconsin, Box 6. Ensign, Bridgman & Fanning circular for *Our Countrymen* in Lossing Collection, Hayes Library, Box 20. One review that this document quoted (accurately) appeared in *Norton's Literary Gazette* 2 (1 June 1855): 231.

14. "C" [Cornelia P. Spencer], "Our Countrymen," *The North-Carolina University Magazine* 4 (September 1855): 305-07; quotation from p. 306. Thanks are due Nancy Pennington for a copy of this review.

15. Lossing to David Swain, 19 November 1855, Swain to Lossing, 24 November 1855, both in the Swain Papers, Southern Historical Collection, University of North Carolina, Chapel Hill.

16. "The True Order of Studies," *Wisconsin Journal of Education* 4 (April 1860), especially p. 305; "P.L.S.," "American History for Schools," *The Western Academician and Journal of Education and Science* 1 (April 1837): 87-90.

17. Sources on Huntington are sparse. I have inferred he was a magazine editor from his 10 November 1853 letter to Lossing, Lossing Collection, Hayes Library, Box 4 in which he asked Lossing to work with him on a "Visitor."

18. Manuscript sources on the delay included: Thomas B. Smith [the printer involved] to Huntington, 8 March 1854, Smith to Lossing, 9 March 1854, Huntington to Lossing, 9 March 1854, all in Lossing Collection, Hayes Library, Box 4; Lossing to Huntington [apparently an unsent draft], 13 March 1854, Lossing Collection, Ibid., Box 1. For later months, see Lossing to Lyman C. Draper, 10 April 1854 and 2 May 1854, both in Draper Correspondence, Box 5; Lossing to Draper, 12 June 1854 and 24 June 1854, Draper Correspondence, Ibid.; Lossing to Draper, 23 December 1854, Draper Correspondence, Ibid., Box 6.

19. J. F. Schroeder to Lossing, 17 October 1854, and M. C. Travy of the Mechanic's Institute School to Lossing, 8 November 1854, both in Lossing Papers, New York Public Library; Lyman C. Draper to Lossing, 18 October 1854 and 31 October 1854, both in Lossing Collection, Syracuse University Library, Box 1. E[dward?] Williams to Lossing, 2 October 1854, Lossing Collection, Hayes Library, Box 8. "Literary Notices," *Harper's* 10 (December 1854): 138.

20. "Editors' Book Table," *The Independent* 6 (26 October 1854): 344.

21. Lossing, *Pictorial History*, p. 311, 311n.

22. Lossing to Swain, 1 November 1854, Swain Papers, Southern Historical Collection, University of North Carolina, Chapel Hill.

23. See E. Kennedy, "Mount Vernon—A Pilgrimage," *Southern Literary Messenger* 18 (January 1852): 53-57; "American Scenes and Incidents. No. III. The Home of Washington," *The New York Journal* 1 (13 August 1853): 104; "Mount Vernon," in Augustus E. Silliman, *A Gallop Among American Scenery* (New-York: D. Appleton & Co., 1853), pp. [13]-24; Erastus Poulson, "The Grave of Washington," in *Our Country: or, The American Parlor Keepsake* (Boston: J. M. Usher, 1854), pp. [133]-42; Erastus Brooks, "Mount Vernon," in *The Wide-Awake Gift: A Know-Nothing Token for 1855* (New York: J. C. Derby [et. al.], 1855), pp. 164-70; C. Collins, D.D., "Mount Vernon," *Ladies' Repository* 17 (March 1857): 163-65. A reaction against what an editor saw as the movement's excesses appeared as "Mount Vernonism," *New York Times*, 25 December 1858, p. 4 col. 6.

24. On Cunningham, see an anonymous pamphlet, *Historical Sketch of Ann Pamela Cunningham* (New York [et. al.]: The Marion Press for the Association, 1929); and Elswyth Thane, *Mount Vernon is Ours: The Story of Its Preservation* (New York: Duell, Sloan and Pearce, 1966). Everett collected his orations in *The Mount Vernon Book* (New York: G. P. Putnam, 1858); see *Historical Magazine* 2 (December 1858): 370.

25. Lossing, *Mount Vernon and Its Associations: Historical, Biographical, and Pictorial* (New York: W. A. Townsend & Company, 1859).

26. S. M. Henry to Lossing, 3 December 1859, Lossing Collection, Historical Society of Pennsylvania. A letter that anticipated Lossing's visit was M. M. Hamilton to Miss Cunningham, 23 April 1859, Early Records of the Mount Vernon Ladies' Association, Mount Vernon Library. On publication, see *Historical Magazine* 3 (July 1859): 228. Commendations of the book included: Cunningham to Lossing, 17 November 1859, LS 536, Lossing Addenda Box 5, Lossing Collection, Huntington Library; William Darlington to Lossing, 23 November 1859, Alexander Brown Papers, College of William and Mary, Box 3 Folder 52.

27. Lossing, *Field-Book of the Revolution* II: pp. 285n.-86n.; *Our Countrymen*, p. 192.

28. My sources on Draper included: William B. Hesseltine, *Pioneer's Mission: The Story of Lyman Copeland Draper* (Madison, Wisc.: State Historical Society of Wisconsin, 1954); and Steven P. Gietschier, "Lyman C. Draper," in *American Historians, 1607-1865*, ed. Clyde N. Wilson, Vol. 30 of *Dictionary of Literary Biography* (Detroit: Gale Research Company, 1984), pp. 68-77. On his work relating to Boone, see John Mack Faragher, *Daniel Boone: The Life and Legend of an American Pioneer* (New York: Henry Holt and Company, 1992), pp. 342-46.

29. Lossing to Draper, 20 March 1854 and 21 March 1854 (apparently sent together), Draper Correspondence, State Historical Society of Wisconsin, Box 4. See also Draper to Lossing, 28 March 1854, Ibid., Box 5; Lossing to Draper, 10 April 1854, Ibid.; Lossing to Draper, 2 May 1854, Ibid.; Lossing Diary, "Brief notes of a trip from Pokeepsie [sic], New York, to Madison, Wisconsin, July, 1854," LS 1117, Lossing Collection, Huntington Library; Lossing-Draper agreement, 19 July 1854, Draper Correspondence, Box 5; Lossing to Draper, 7 December 1855, Ibid., Box 7.

30. Among expressions of interest in Boone, see Samuel Lorenzo Knapp, *Lectures on American Literature* (orig. ed. 1829), reprinted as *American Cultural History 1607-1829* (Delmar, N.Y.: Scholars' Facsimiles & Reprints, 1977), pp. 260-263; "The Pioneers of Kentucky," *North American Review* 62 (January 1846): 71-101. The competing book that concerned Lossing and Draper most was W. H. Bogart, *Daniel Boone and the Hunters of Kentucky* (Auburn, N.Y. and Buffalo: Miller, Orton & Mulligan, 1854 and later editions). Lossing, at least, claimed to not consider Bogart a serious rival. See Lossing to Draper, 21 September 1854, Draper Correspondence, Box 6. Other related books included: Henry C. Watson, *Six Nights in a Block-House; or, Sketches of Border Life* (Philadelphia: John E. Potter and Company, 1851), especially pp. 91-132; [Francis L. Hawks], *The Adventures of Daniel Boone, The Kentucky Rifleman* (New York: D. Appleton & Co. [et.al.], 1854); the text of that book also appeared as *Life of Daniel Boone* (Dayton, Ohio: Ells, Marquis & Company, 1856).

31. The earliest reference I found was "New Life of Col. Daniel Boone," a clipping from the [Madison, Wis.] *Daily Argus and Democrat*, 13 May [1854], Lossing Collection, Hayes Library, Box 11. One New York notice was important since many other magazines and newspapers reprinted it: "Literary Intelligence. A Literary Partnership," *Norton's Literary Gazette and Publishers' Circular* n.s. 1 (17 September 1854): 441-42. A North Carolina column, apparently from David Swain's pen, derived from that in *Norton's*: "Literary Intelligence. A Literary Partnership—Interesting Works," *Southern Weekly Post* 3 (28 October 1854): 187. See also "Literary Notices," *Harper's* 9 (November, 1854): 860. Horatio Gates Jones to Lossing, 12 November 1855, Lossing Collection, Hayes Library, Box 5; Parkman to Draper, 2 June 1857,

Draper Correspondence, reprinted in *Letters of Francis Parkman*, ed. Wilbur R. Jacobs (Norman, Okla.: University of Oklahoma Press, 1960), I: 128.

32. One published work was Lossing's article, "Daniel Boone," *Harper's* 19 (October 1859): [577]-601.

33. Lossing to Draper, 28 August 1854, Draper Correspondence, Box 6; Draper to Lossing, 17 December 1854, Lossing Collection, Syracuse University Library, Box 1; Lossing to Draper, 28 December 1859, Draper Correspondence, Box 11.

34. Draper, *King's Mountain and Its Heroes* (Cincinnati: Peter G. Thomson, 1881).

35. Lossing to Draper, 22 October 1854, Draper Correspondence, Box 6. See also, among many relevant manuscripts: Lossing to Samuel G. Arnold, 18 January 1855 and 10 February 1855, Arnold Papers, Virginia Historical Society; Lossing to Dr. John W. Francis, 3 February, 1855, Lossing Collection, Syracuse University Library, Box 3; Lossing to G. P. Morris, 22 February 1855, Lamport Manuscripts, Box 1, folder 65, Yale University Library; Lossing to Evert Duyckinck, 7 March 1855, Duyckinck Collection, New York Public Library; Lossing to Fletcher Harper, 17 March 1855, Harper Collection, Pierpont Morgan Library; Lossing to J. F. Schroeder, 27 March 1855, LS 1145, Lossing Addenda Box 3, Lossing Collection, Huntington Library; Lossing to Draper, 19 April 1855, Draper Correspondence, Box 6. A clipping of an obituary for Alice from the *Charleston [NY?] Courier*, 27 April 1855, was in the Lossing Collection, Hayes Library, Box 17. On the spa visits, see Lossing to Draper, 6 July 1855, Draper Correspondence, Box 6.

36. Helen Lossing Diary, Call No. 17940, New York State Library; "The Lossing Family-Book," Lossing Collection, Hayes Library, Box 1; Lossing to Mrs. Lossing, 23 September 1857, Lossing Collection, Syracuse University Library, Box 1; Lossing Journal, LS 1120, Lossing Collection, Huntington Library.

37. Lossing to Charles Campbell, 1 April 1858, Campbell Papers, College of William and Mary. Lossing's time in Dutchess County gave him opportunities to grow active in Poughkeepsie's Episcopal Christ Church; he twice served as a Vestryman and once represented the parish at the state Diocese Convention. *The Records of Christ Church: Poughkeepsie, New York*, ed. Helen Wilkinson Reynolds (Poughkeepsie, N.Y.: Frank B. Howard, 1911), pp. 306, 308.

38. See the Draper Correspondence, Box 42.

39. Hudson Taylor to Lossing, 29 January 1851, June Collection of the War of 1812, Oberlin College Library, describing a Washington, D.C., monument to sailors who served in the 1804 Tripolian conflict.

40. Horatio G. Jones, Jr. to Lossing, 16 January 1852, Alexander Brown Papers, College of William and Mary, Box 3, folder 53. Lossing's 1852 correspondence on the 1812 project was voluminous; one of the crucial documents was a printed circular that he sent to persons he thought might possess information. Over the next decade he used copies of this letter, redating it as appropriate. One copy that Lossing amended to read "Oct. 1854," apparently so he could continue to circulate it, was in the Lossing Collection, Hayes Library, Box 1.

41. Lossing to Alice [Mrs. Lossing], 4 March 1853, Lossing Addenda Box 3, Lossing Collection, Huntington Library. Lossing to F[letcher] Harper, 5 March 1853, Harper Collection, Pierpont Morgan Library. Sources on the final contract included: Lossing to Harper & Bros., 28 November 1859, Lossing Collection, Hayes Library, Box 1; Harpers to Lossing, 30 November 1859, Ibid., Box 4 (copies of both documents were in the Harper Collection, Pierpont Morgan Library); Lossing-Harpers Contract,

20 December 1859, Harpers Archives, Reel 1: Contract Books, Vol. 1 p. 374, and reel 53: Correspondence Relating to Contracts, from Box 18 in original.

42. Manuscript copies of this circular were in the Lossing Collection, Syracuse University Library, Box 3, and Miscellaneous: Lossing materials, New-York Historical Society. A printed version appeared in "Literary," *Harper's Weekly* 4 (18 February 1860): 102.

43. Lossing to Samuel G. Arnold, 26 January 1860, Arnold Papers, Virginia Historical Society. On the actual trip, see especially two Lossing letters, both dated 15 August 1860: to Mrs. Lossing, Lossing Collection, Hayes Library, Box 1; to Thurlow Weed, Weed Papers, University of Rochester Library. See also Lossing to Mrs. Lossing, 21 September 1860, Lossing Collection, Syracuse University Library, Box 1.

44. Stephen Champlain to Lossing, 3 November 1860, June Collection of the War of 1812, Oberlin College Library.

45. Simms to Lossing, 13 December 1860, A. C. Goodyear Manuscripts, vol. 4, p. 6, Yale University.

46. Lossing to Mrs. Lossing, 23 December 1860, Lossing Collection, Syracuse University Library, Box 1.

7

PATRIOTIC LORE: LOSSING'S CIVIL WAR

The Civil War and the sectional crises associated with it inspired Americans from various backgrounds to explore the conflict's meaning. Political, religious, social, and other themes overlapped as writers tried to relate the war to national history. Lossing's major work in this genre, his *Pictorial History of the Civil War*,[1] illustrates this generalization. For Lossing, writing a history of the Civil War presented an opportunity to record new traditions of patriotic lore for Americans' edification. It also forced Lossing to reevaluate his earlier views on the meaning of the national past.

Almost all scholars have ignored this work, not without reason. More than any other of Lossing's productions, the *Pictorial History* conveyed a single interpretation without a hint that other viewpoints possessed validity; the Union cause was almost totally good and the Confederate even more completely evil. Yet the history of Lossing's writings on the Civil War offers insights on the production and uses of contemporary history in nineteenth-century American culture.

Before Abraham Lincoln's presidential election precipitated the secession of South Carolina and other slave states, Lossing made few references to his personal opinions about slavery or sectional tensions. In 1859, he did perceive sectional reconciliation as necessary for preserving national ideals. In a rare expression of political allegiance, he admitted pride in giving his vote to "the anti-sectional and conservative party, called Republican." A week before the election, Lossing took heart in Lincoln's likely victory. "I rejoice at the prospect of a change in the policy of our government, by the election of an honest man to the presidency."[2]

Ironically, Lossing's first confrontation with the "Rebellion" came from his efforts to investigate an unrelated topic. During the secession winter of 1860-61, Lossing made a trip to the South for research on the War of 1812.

After the fall of Fort Sumter, he tarried in New Orleans until he felt compelled to flee north "for fear of hot times[.]"[3] Lossing returned through Kentucky where he felt relief in seeing the national flag. Crossing Ohio and Pennsylvania, Lossing took heart in those states' displays of patriotism.[4]

Early suggestions that Lossing might write the war's history came as friends remarked on the crisis and hinted that it provided a worthy if frightful theme for his talents. Frederic Kidder, an antiquarian who later toured battlefields with Lossing, offered one explicit statement. "Does not the present condition of our country look gloomy beyond any former period," he commented. "It may yet be your duty to write the history of 'the Decline & Fall of the American Union[.]'"[5]

Through 1861, Lossing still focussed on research about the War of 1812 rather than the Civil War.[6]   He did so because, like many other others, he thought the war could not last long. But friends and publishers did not always concur and urged Lossing to write on "this present war." Historian George W. Greene suggested in September that Lossing would lose readers if he delayed, and so "must hurry on to be ready for a 'Field Book' of the Rebellion."[7]

In December 1861, a Philadelphia publisher, George W. Childs, presented Lossing with the most serious proposal for such a work. Quickly Lossing responded to Childs that "I am as confident as yourself that a superbly illustrated book on *The Great Rebellion*, similar to my *Field-Book of the Revolution*, would be very successful as 'a literary and commercial enterprise', in our hands." Not wishing to surrender all credit for the idea, he noted that "[i]t has been my intention, from the beginning of the Rebellion, to make such a record of it as would, as it were, exhaust the subject, and make it a standard authority forever. . . . I wish to be so thorough that no one will attempt the task, *in the same way*."[8]

Early in 1862, Childs and Lossing agreed on specifics of the project. Lossing was to furnish a complete manuscript with his suggestions for illustrations, while Childs bore all remaining costs. Lossing estimated that he could complete the work in a volume of 800 to 900 pages. Childs quickly accepted these terms and within a week reported considerable public interest in Lossing's project. "I am constantly getting letters from all quarters in regard to the great book. I hope we may all be spared to see its completion. It will be your lasting monument."[9]

Soon Childs's enthusiasm soared as he assembled endorsements of Lossing's book from scores of public figures. The earliest dated letter, from Edward Everett, cited Lossing's past successes—especially the *Field-Book of the Revolution*—as evidence that further historical conquests were certain. "Mr. Lossing's diligence in exploring the localities which he describes, his fidelity and accuracy as an historian, and the spirit of his illustrations, are too well known, from his volumes which are already before the public, to need any recommendation." Similarly glowing comments came from such luminaries as Oliver Wendell Holmes, Sr., William Cullen Bryant, and Jared Sparks. Others wrote directly to Lossing; "yours will be the Clarendon of this 'Great Rebellion,'" one contact predicted.[10]

But Lossing did not rest on such praise. His plans for the project reached an advanced stage by March 1862, when he described them to Francis Lieber, then a Columbia College professor and a close friend. Lossing recalled his practice in the first *Field-Book*, noting that he had introduced few detailed battle descriptions there. Similarly, "[i]n my work on the Rebellion, I shall introduce no battle scenes, unless I shall find something of the kind necessary to illustrate an important fact." He granted the difficulty of his task and worried that he might not prove equal to it. "With the greatest sincerity, I say that I approach the subject with a feeling of the greatest responsibility. It is emphatically *the* Great Rebellion in History, and to transmit to posterity a faithful record of the Event, is a task of great magnitude and importance."[11]

Meanwhile, Childs reported "working like a beaver" on the project. He estimated that he could get 500 agents for selling the book door-to-door and planned other means to make the public aware of it. "I shall have ample opportunity of advertising it in my new books." Later Childs noted the flood of applicants who wanted to sell the book. "They all think it will be the book of the age. So do I!"[12]

Later the perspectives of both publisher and writer grew less sanguine, mainly due to one decision: Childs and Lossing chose not to publish the book until after the war ended. This resolution, which from later scholars' viewpoints seems obviously proper, caused the pair concern as others filled the market with histories that, while fragmentary, enjoyed wide sales.[13] As Lossing remarked, "[t]he publisher is naturally a little nervous, because several other publishers have announced histories of the rebellion[.]" But Lossing thought his reasons for waiting were compelling. "I hope to record the great state trials that will follow [the war], and the thorough finishing up of this dark chapter in our history, by the execution of the leading conspirators." More than Childs, Lossing remained untroubled by competing histories. "Others may 'take the top of the market' . . . . These [books] must be ephemeral. *I* wish to make a work for all time, and I think the publisher's wishes will in the end be better satisfied."[14]

Other parties fretted over the situation, including applicants for book-selling agencies. One correspondent explicitly mentioned Lossing's competition in maintaining that "I fear you are delaying your work on the rebellion to a late day. Abbot[']s book has been distributed in this region & I suppose elsewhere, & as it is a large work, I fear you will find it in your way."[15]

Childs expressed similar concerns. Sometimes he could only vent frustration at readers' impatience. "War literature is all the rage now. The meanest of the 'Histories of the Rebellion' are having large sales. It is really astonishing how little our people know &, it is singular that they should purchase these trashy works." Later he regained enough optimism to assert that an attractive initial volume would assure "great success" for Lossing's work.[16] But Childs's worries remained.

Later in 1863, Childs developed more precise plans for Lossing's opus. A multi-volume work of the English historian Charles Knight became his model in terms of format. "I suppose you have Knight[']s Popular History of England. It is my idea of a taking work. Your History published somewhat in the same style and manner would be just the thing for our people." He discussed how to organize and price Lossing's work, which he wanted to sell via subscriptions. Childs recognized that the history would require several volumes and speculated that five or six might prove necessary. "As soon as we could get *one volume out* we could at once secure the market. . . . I feel it is a 'big thing' and if properly managed is a fortune for author and publisher." Childs grew anxious that Lossing should write the first installment quickly. "The sooner we can get out the first vol[ume] . . the better for us. Is it impossible for you to go ahead on this vol[ume]?"[17]

Lossing did "go ahead" in contacting federal officials and private citizens for documents and recollections and started to sift through this material. A newspaper column noted his hard work "collecting and arranging ample materials for his great work on the Rebellion." Lossing also travelled, e.g., to Pennsylvania in July 1863, soon after federal forces repelled Robert E. Lee at Gettysburg. From Harrisburg a few days after the battle, he noted rumors "that few if any of Lee's army will recross the Potomac—not enough, at any rate, to form . . . any considerable force." George Meade's Army of the Potomac had "struck the Rebellion in a vital part. Henceforth we shall see only its death struggles." But although the war now seemed in its last stages, Lossing remained convinced that "I have before me a great and most important work. . . . Never was a more dignified and responsible task laid upon the energies of a man."[18]

Indeed, Lossing filled the next twenty months with a plethora of research endeavors on the War. After Lincoln's 1864 re-election, with Union victory in sight, Lossing expanded his efforts. In December 1864 he joined General Benjamin Butler and a fleet that bombarded Fort Fisher, North Carolina. He also toured Union-controlled areas of Virginia. In support of that venture, General Lew Wallace, a long-time friend of Lossing, wrote an introductory letter to Ulysses S. Grant. In it Wallace implied that Grant should help Lossing because the history would record Grant's brilliant military career. "He will have a great deal to do with you, and the many noble things you have done; it is well enough, General, that you should know him."[19]

In April 1865, as the Army of the Potomac surrounded and captured Lee's army in Virginia, Lossing planned a trip to the heart of the action. A friend in Alexandria cautioned him that "*Moseby [sic] the noted guerilla*" still made travel to some localities dangerous. Still, "I have no dout [sic] the military would grant you every facility in their power to visit these places[.]" After Lee's surrender, another correspondent came near reading Lossing's mind: "I suppose you will soon visit Richmond & Petersburgh [sic] where you will find a full month[']s work for your Pen & Pencil." Within a few days Lossing did go to Richmond, from whence he hauled off boxes of Confederate records and other materials. As he told his wife, "[w]hat I had already procured, and shall still further procure, will repay me ten[-]fold for the time and money spent. I cannot tell you what I have got. I will only say that I have most precious treasures."[20]

As Lossing settled down to write his first volume, he and Childs remained in dialogue about the proper interpretation to present. Childs tried to persuade Lossing to tone down his pro-Union rhetoric in the manuscript. "As our book will be the only one that will be likely to have any sale in the [S]outh I think it would be well to keep down as much as is consistent all personal feeling, and endeavor to give as fair and honest a statement as possible in regard to both sides." Childs argued "that thousands of honest men south thought they had a right to go out of the Union. I want as far as possible to avoid a *bitterness* of feeling towards the South, as they have been whipped and admit it and seem disposed to endeavor to do right in the future." Seeking to not upset Lossing, his plea merged cosmic and commercial motives. "Do not think me officious but believe I have only the good of mankind and the success of your book at heart in all that I have hastily written."

Lossing's reply has not survived, but in it he evidently reacted to the implied criticism, since soon Childs penned another anxious note. He apologized for any offense, re-explaining the need for moderate language with aid from Lossing's own words. Finally Childs granted that Lossing was, after all, the only proper judge of his own work. "Write the History just as your good sense and honest judgment dictate and I will not say a word in the future as I know no man is more anxious to be just."[21]

Early in 1866, Childs announced the imminent publication of Lossing's first volume, carrying his narrative through the First Battle of Bull Run. It actually appeared in June.[22] The delay did not dampen the praise that readers extended to Lossing. A New Hampshire friend remarked that "[s]o far as you have gone in your 'Chronicle,' the candor & impartiality, the love of truth, justice & liberty of the writer, are as conspicuous as his [sic] abhorrence of hypocrisy, falsehood, injustice & oppression."[23]

Most periodicals voiced similar perspectives. The New York *Herald* labeled Volume One "the first conscientiously written history of the war that has been given to the world since its close. It is neither one-sided as to its facts nor as to its conclusions." *Godey's* found the book judicious. "From its pages a stranger to the great contest might readily gather all that is necessary to the comprehension of the causes that brought about rebellion, and the motives of the Southern leaders. . . . We do not doubt that the succeeding volumes will justify the high expectations to which this first has given rise." A Vermont newspaper compared the work favorably with *The Field-Book of the Revolution* and predicted that it would soon "take position beside its predecessor as one of the indispensable books for a well[-]filled Library."[24]

An important source for ideas for Lossing through his first and second installments was Francis Lieber. In the immediate post-war years, Lieber, who had recently gained a post as curator of captured Confederate records, became a prominent advocate of a more nationalistic orientation. He saw this as overcoming the errors of state-rights ideology. Besides the motivation of his friendship with Lossing, Lieber wanted to encourage the *Pictorial History* as a vehicle for furthering his vision of American political life.[25]

Meanwhile, Lossing filled 1866 with various research efforts. His major activity was an ambitious round of visits to battlefields and other sites, similar to his efforts for the *Field-Book of the Revolution*. During the trips, he sketched the places and interviewed participants from both sides. A March 1866 letter to Childs, which also served as a solicitation for documents or memoirs, represented Lossing's most explicit itinerary for these travels; apparently, he held to it over the next seven months.

Starting down the Atlantic coast from Washington, Lossing visited points between Roanoke Island and Savannah. Then he went inland through Macon, Atlanta, Chattanooga (pausing at the Shiloh battlefield), Corinth, Mississippi, and Mobile. A steamship trip to New Orleans opened Louisiana, Arkansas, and Missouri to Lossing. From St. Louis, he descended the Mississippi to Cairo, Island No. 10, Memphis, and Nashville. A return to Chattanooga was the starting point for a swing over the mountains into Virginia, where Lossing traced the campaigns of McClellan and Grant. Finally, with visits to battlefields at South Mountain, Antietam, and Gettysburg, Lossing estimated the he covered 20,000 miles for the *Pictorial History*.[26]

While initial sales pleased Childs, he nonetheless realized they were not as high as he had hoped. Soon Childs reached the conclusion that other businesses—especially his Philadelphia newspaper, the *Public Ledger*—would not allow proper concentration on the *Pictorial History*. In 1867, with Lossing's first volume only briefly in circulation, Childs transferred publication rights to Timothy Belknap and Co. of Hartford, a firm that had ties to that city's American Publishing Company. Lossing and Childs parted business company but remained friends, as evidenced by positive things Lossing wrote about Childs in a Centennial book a decade later.[27]

The decision to transfer publishing rights involved various turns. Lossing wanted to give D. Appleton & Co. of Philadelphia first chance at the

Pictorial History, but that firm rebuffed him. In April 1867, Lossing sounded out another Hartford company about taking over the work, unaware that they already had a multi-volume work on the Civil War in their charge. In making that offer, he disclosed that in the ten months since publication, Childs had sold 6,000 of the 10,000 copies of the first volume's first edition. Lossing thought this showed his work's potential for high sales.[28]

Local agents did not always echo such optimism, even after the new publisher came on board. Some worried that Belknap's unfamiliarity with the subscription market might diminish the work's success: "[t]he number trade is something new to our Hartford people and I imagine they are fearful that the success of the Book in that form will not warrant the additional expense." Another fretted over the need to publish Volume Two quickly. "I have something over two hundred orders for Civil War in America. . . . [But] I fear that I shall loose [sic] a good many orders on account of the delay."[29]

The *Pictorial History's* second volume appeared in November 1867 and, according to one source, enjoyed good sales.[30] Lossing barely had time to record the event, since writing the work's third and final section required all his energy. As he told Evert Duyckinck, "[m]y *History of the Civil War* is not finished, and until I write the last line of that I suppose I may not expect leisure." Even in February 1868, Lossing reported himself "[v]ery busy in my History of Civil War. Worked on it till about 11 o'clock in the Evening."[31]

In the spring of 1868, Lossing's final volume appeared. Belknap took steps to publicize it, buying advertisements in three hundred newspapers. His efforts evidently failed, since by year's end he fretted that sales were not meeting his expectations. Even the expedient of renaming the *Pictorial History* as a *Field-Book* to exploit the fame of Lossing's other work proved unavailing.[32] As was the case earlier, Lossing felt that publication delays were the reason Volume Three did not enjoy better sales.[33]

Meanwhile periodical reviewers practically ignored the *History's* second and third volumes, frustrating efforts to give the books wide publicity. The American reading public, eager to read about the war while it continued, grew sated with such books within a few years of the conflict's end. Ambitious works such as Lossing's fared especially poorly, except when their writers possessed more intellectual distinction (as in John William Draper's case) or political importance (like Horace Greeley) than he.[34] Lossing's well-intentioned delay left his herculean research and writing efforts unrewarded. As in other episodes, Lossing displayed a real if naive desire to offer a serious work but insufficient business sense to recognize the slimness of his resultant chances for commercial success.

Despite Lossing's determination to write better history by waiting until war's end, when the *Pictorial History* did appear its interpretations repeated those of northern books that appeared during the conflict. Like other writers, Lossing traced the war's origins to a "slave-power conspiracy;" he was only marginally less extreme than others in depicting that plot as a central fact of American history.[35]   Amendments to the *History*'s manuscript show that Lossing originally wanted to make references to the slave-power even more frequent.[36]

Like others, Lossing mentioned the rebellion's historical roots. He thought the slaveholders' plot had evolved since the 1780s. "That conspiracy budded when the Constitution of the Republic became the supreme law of the land, and, under the culture of disloyal and ambitious men, after gradual development and long ripening, assumed the form and substance of a rebellion of a few arrogant land and slaveholders against popular government. It was the rebellion of an OLIGARCHY against the PEOPLE, with whom the sovereign power is rightfully lodged." History demonstrated "that rebellion and civil war were logical results of the increasing activity of potential antagonisms, controlled and energized by selfish men for selfish purposes." The slaveholders' aristocracy thus shouldered total blame for the conflict. "Because the majority of the people of the United States would not consent to abase the Constitution, and make it subservient to the cause of injustice and inhumanity, the Oligarchy rebelled and kindled a horrible civil war!" (I: [17]-18, 63, 220).

In his final chapter, Lossing offered his most extended speculations on the war's meaning. His argument was that the conflict's outcome offered assurance that republican government would triumph. "The important political problem of the nineteenth century was solved by our Civil War. Our Republic no longer appeared as an *experiment*, but as a *demonstration*." He depicted the contest as "a struggle between ideas of the dead past and those of the living present—between wrong and right in their broadest and most conspicuous aspects. It resulted in the utter extinction of slavery, and in the establishment of the Republic, with a Constitution purified and strengthened, upon the eternal foundations of Truth and Justice."(III: 584, 613). These remarks gave Lossing occasion to comprehend the Civil War within broader perspectives on the nation's past, present, and future.

Such ideas were not new. Although Lossing delayed publishing his history, he did not wait to reach personal convictions about the Civil War. At first, his beliefs mainly involved references to Providence working through the war, a common viewpoint among contemporary northerners. "I have had unswerving faith in three beings, in connection with the Rebellion, namely, General McClellan, President Lincoln and the Lord of Hosts. I have believed, from the beginning, that the hand of the Almighty was to be put forth, at this time, so tangibly in the chastisement, strengthening, and purification of this nation, that the most stupid and skeptical observer must perceive God in the history of our day."[37]

Lossing's Providentialism grew more precise in late 1862, when Lincoln's Emancipation Proclamation linked the Union cause to slavery's destruction. Now the war promised to fulfill American ideals of bringing freedom to all peoples. "What a glorious future God is preparing for our beloved country!" Lossing exclaimed. As 1862 ended and the Proclamation came near taking effect, Lossing exulted over the dawning day of freedom. "I should raise the 'stars and stripes' over my house on the first of January," he commented. "That will be a white day in the calendar of our beloved country[.]"[38]

A crucial factor in Lossing and his friends shedding this cheerful perspective was the question of post-war federal policy toward the South. In worrying over Reconstruction, Lossing and others recognized, especially after Andrew Johnson succeeded the slain Lincoln as President, that on the issue of political and racial readjustment, the North might lose the fruits of its hard-won victory. By the War's third summer, Lossing developed a theory of how the North could bring the late Confederate states into the Union at war's end. Writing to the *New York Times*, he offered a perspective on reconstruction that paralleled the Lincoln Administration's. He held that complete restructuring of the South's political system was unnecessary because the states' constitutions, though now dormant because rebellious elements had commandeered governmental functions, would come back into effect as each came under Federal control. "As the rebellion shall be crushed out in State after State, . . . [each state] will resume its local powers [and] commence immediately working harmoniously with the National Government as before the rebellion. There can be no such thing as 'coming back'—no 'reconstruction,' but simply a resumption of now dormant powers."

Lossing reiterated the pointlessness of debate over the southern states' constitutional status, at least while fighting continued. "I believe discussions about 'reconstruction' to be not only idle and unnecessary, but absolutely mischievous, because they produce confusion and divert our attention from the great and only business of the patriot to-day, which is to *crush the rebellion*. Do that and the perfect Union will speedily reappear in more than its former splendor." Sending a copy of the letter to Secretary of State William Seward, Lossing expressed hopes that his ideas could serve as a rallying point for loyal Americans. "The true friends of the Republic must have a few simple, cardinal principles, which may not yield to expediency, to rest upon in the great debate which is to follow the disbanding of armies when the rebellion shall be crushed. Let us find them, comprehend them, and then let there be perfect accord among the champions of right, of whom you are foremost."[39]

The difficulty of maintaining this agenda grew apparent after Lincoln's death, as Andrew Johnson inherited the presidential chair. When Johnson won the Vice Presidency in late 1864, Lossing wrote to him, soliciting information about disunion in Johnson's native Tennessee. Lossing included a postscript that suggested his attitude toward Johnson at that time: "Allow me to express my profound gratitude to God for the Election of Mr[.] Lincoln and yourself, to the highest chairs of State." After Lincoln died,

Lossing felt a spasm of grief and shock, although he expressed confidence that Johnson would perform capably and that the nation would thrive under his direction.[40] This confidence proved short-lived.

In 1866, Lossing grew convinced that Johnson was far too lenient toward the South. Johnson granted pardons to practically all former Confederate officials and soldiers and urged the quick readmittance of southern Congressional delegations, resisting Republicans who wanted to make protection of Blacks a condition for that step. The exact date of Lossing's disenchantment remains unclear, but by mid-1866, he had lost all respect for Johnson.[41]

After Henry Ward Beecher published a letter supporting Johnson, Lossing wrote a censure to Beecher, expressing disappointment in him and distrust for Johnson. Lossing alluded to Johnson's speaking tour in search of support, calling him

that dangerous public enemy now going through the country inciting Civil War, and, by his indecorous and blasphemous language, shocking the sensibilities of every Patriot and Christian, corrupting the fountains of public morals, and bringing disgrace . . . upon the exalted office into which the red hand of a murderer lifted him. I solemnly believe him to be in secret league with the enemies of the Republic . . . [and] preparing the way for a bold stroke for a Dictatorship.[42]

In 1868, Lossing's disgust climaxed. As Johnson's battle with Congress ended in the President's impeachment, Lossing's diary included a running commentary on Johnson's sordid character, with expressions of hope for his removal from office. As Congress assembled in January, Lossing reiterated his conviction that Johnson "is a vulgar Demagogue, of slave-labor State birth, [and] of intemperate habits." When the President tried to remove War Secretary Edwin Stanton for Stanton's sympathies with Congressional Republicans, Lossing commented that "Johnson is a great Villain and a curse to the country. He ought to be deposed at once." A week afterward, Lossing could scarcely contain his glee when Stanton's removal had apparently destroyed Johnson's political base and made his fall inevitable. "Few Democrats, so called, care whether he is removed from office or not. His vulgarity and wickedness is too much even for that corrupt and disloyal party to bear. He will go into obscurity, followed by the contempt of every decent person[.]"[43]   But that spring, the Senate held Johnson's impeachment trial and narrowly voted not to remove him from office.

Johnson's acquittal disappointed Lossing, although other political developments revived his hopes for the defeat of Democratic, state-rights interests. Thus as the 1868 presidential campaign reached its close, the Democrats remained in disarray and the Republicans stood poised to retain Federal control, as they indeed did with Ulysses S. Grant's victory. With American nationalism ascending, Lossing enthused to Francis Lieber about the country's prospects. "To me the skies of the future of our Country appears [sic] very bright. I believe the Republican vote will be so over-whelming, that it will silence Rebellion, forever."[44]

This overt nationalism represented one of the Civil War's major legacies for Lossing. In earlier decades, his writings contained little discussion of the Union's nature, perhaps because he perceived that emergent sectional tensions rendered this topic too controversial. The Civil War ended Lossing's fears on that score. Although he recognized that the Republicans' political triumph could prove fleeting, the North's military victory made national survival and political unity certain. In following years, Lossing displayed far greater willingness to recognize political conflicts and even take sides in them, especially controversies with sectional components.

Such views notwithstanding, in the late 1860s Lossing may have been uncertain that the nationalism he and others espoused would indeed triumph in American life. This concern motivated him to use later writings to buttress these ideas. Indeed, this aim persisted through the remaining twenty years of his career. Lossing's desire to solidify the Civil War's results grew especially prominent in the work that represented his greatest contribution to historical literature: the *Pictorial Field-Book of the War of 1812*, published in 1868.

NOTES

1. Lossing, *Pictorial History of the Civil War in the United States of America*. Vol. 1 (Philadelphia: George W. Childs, 1866); Vols. 2-3 (Hartford: T. Belknap and Co., 1867-68).

2. Lossing to Lyman C. Draper, 6 December 1859, Draper Correspondence, State Historical Society of Wisconsin, Box 11; Lossing to Samuel G. Arnold, 31 October 1860, Arnold Papers, Virginia Historical Society.

3. Manuscripts on this trip's earlier stages included: Harper & Bros. to H. D. McGinness, 14 December 1860, LS 796, Lossing Addenda Box 6, Lossing Collection, Huntington Library; Lossing to Unidentified, 4 January 1860 [sic; should read 1861], Lossing Collection, Syracuse University Library, Box 3; Brantz Mayer to Lossing, 21 January 1861, Lossing Collection, Syracuse University Library, Box 1. Lossing's notes from the trip, LS 1132, were in the Lossing Collection, Huntington Library. The "hot times" quote came from Lossing to Mrs. Lossing, 16 April 1861, LS 1177, Lossing Addenda Box 7, Huntington Library. A New Orleans newspaper noticed Lossing's presence approvingly: *Daily Picayune*, 12 April 1861, Morning Edition, p. 4 col. 1.

4. A column on a New-York Historical Society meeting recorded Lossing's comment on the flag: *Historical Magazine* 5 (June 1861): 178. On Lossing's homeward journey, see especially his 25 April 1861 letter to William H. Seward from Pittsburgh, Seward Papers, University of Rochester Library. Lossing also described his experiences in the South for some Poughkeepsie newspapers: see the clipping "Travels and Observations in the South," *The Daily Press* n.d. [ca. May, 1861?], Lossing Collection, Hayes Library, Box 15. W. Schram asked Lossing to write that paper; Schram to Lossing, 27 April 1861, Lossing Papers, Adriance Memorial Library, Poughkeepsie.

Other clippings were in the Lossing Collection, Hayes Library, Box 15: "Friends of the South," *Poughkeepsie Daily Eagle*, 7 May 1861, and a letter responding to "South[-]Side View of the Question of Slavery," *Poughkeepsie Telegraph*, 7 September 1861.

5. Kidder to Lossing, 10 January 1861, Lossing Collection, Duke University. A similar comment appeared in C. C. Savage to Lossing, 15 January 1861, Lossing Collection, Hayes Library, Box 7. Horatio Jones, Jr. of the Historical Society of Pennsylvania reached similar conclusions but made some bizarre political remarks. "What a sad condition we are in as a free government—It is a *free* one with a vengeance. 'Liberty run mad—' We need a Louis Napoleon for a few months on this Continent—I very much fear that er you close your war of 1812—you will have to mend your pen to write that of 1861." Jones to Lossing, 11 January 1861, Alexander Brown Papers, College of William and Mary, Box 3, folder 53. John E. Wool to Lossing, 16 May 1861, LS 2108, Lossing Addenda Box 8, Lossing Collection, Huntington Library. Wool, a Troy, New York resident and an Army General far past his prime, took Lossing's role as the war's chronicler seriously enough to favor him with a 30-page defense of recent military decisions. [Wool] to Lossing, June 1861, Lossing Collection, Syracuse University Library, Box 1.

6. He went to Washington, D.C., in November, but concentrated on work about the War of 1812. I first saw a diary of this visit in the Lossing Collection, Syracuse University Library, Box 4; the diary was a copy of an original at Vassar College. The original is in Box 6 of Vassar's Lossing Collection. This recorded that he saw George W. Childs, later the publisher of Volume One of Lossing's Civil War history, in Philadelphia.

7. He told Lyman C. Draper that he expected the government to crush the Confederacy by year's end. Then, he hoped, the Lincoln Administration would insure peace by outlawing slavery and so uprooting the South's ruling class. Lossing to Draper, 20 August 1861, Draper Correspondence, State Historical Society of Wisconsin, Box 13. Hurlbut, Williams & Co. to Lossing, 18 February [sic] 1861, Lossing Collection, Hayes Library, Box 1. The apparent reference to "this present war" months before the firing on Ft. Sumter suggests that this manuscript's date might have been an error (1862?). Greene to Lossing, 14 September 1861, Lossing Collection, Hayes Library, Box 4.

8. Lossing to Childs, 21 December 1861, Lossing Collection, Hayes Library, Box 1. On Childs, see James Parton, *George W. Childs: A Biographical Sketch* (Philadelphia: Collins, 1870); Jacqueline Steck's article in *American Newspaper Journalists, 1873-1900* ed. Perry J. Ashley, Vol. 23 of *Dictionary of Literary Biography* (Detroit: Gale Research Company, 1983), pp. 26-30; and John Tebbel, *A History of Book Publishing in the United States. Volume I: The Creation of an Industry 1630-1865* (New York & London: R. R. Bowker, 1972), pp. 378-82.

9. Lossing to Childs, 6 January 1862, Lossing Collection, Hayes Library, Box 1; Childs to Lossing, 12 January 1862, LS 463, Lossing Addenda Box 8, Lossing Collection, Huntington Library.

10. Printed copies or extracts from these letters were in the Lossing Collection, Hayes Library, Boxes 15 and 20. The small Childs Collection, Syracuse University Library, contained the originals of several endorsements; the printed versions were direct quotes from them. Eventually Childs assembled over 200 endorsements for his Lossing project. See George Ticknor to Childs, 22 March 1862, Berg Collection, New York Public Library; W. B. Sprague to Childs, 26 April 1862, Alexander Brown Papers,

College of William Mary, Box 3, folder 57; Lewis Cass to Childs, 30 April 1862, Miscellaneous Manuscripts—Cass, Lewis, New-York Historical Society. S. Austin Allibone to Lossing, 6 January 1862, Lossing Collection, Historical Society of Pennsylvania. See also the untitled notice in the Philadelphia *Press*, 7 April 1862, p. [2] col. 2; Robert R. Corson included a clipping of this in his letter to Lossing, 7 April 1862, Schoff Civil War Collection: Diaries and Journals, William Clements Library, University of Michigan. "Miscellany," a column in the *Historical Magazine*, mentioned the project twice: 6 (June 1862): 200; *Historical Magazine* (November 1862): 360. In late 1864, readers were still recalling *The Field-Book of the Revolution* as evidence that the new work should succeed. Washington Hunt to Lossing, 18 November 1864, New York State Library, Call No. 7244.

11. Lossing to Lieber, 27 March 1862, LI 2681, Lieber Collection, same repository.

12. Childs letters to Lossing, 2 April 1862 and 19 May 1862, LS 466 and LS 469, respectively, both in Lossing Addenda Box 8, Lossing Collection, same repository.

13. "Notes on Books," *Historical Magazine* 9 (November 1865): 354.

14. Lossing to Lieber, 27 March 1862, LI 2681, Lieber Collection, Huntington Library.

15. J. Emmins to Lossing, 23 May 1862, Lossing Collection, Syracuse University Library, Box 1; Tho. B. Fairchild to Lossing, 2 April 1863, LS 640, Lossing Addenda Box 9, Lossing Collection, Huntington Library. Fairchild was referring to the first volume of John S. C. Abbott, *The History of the Civil War in America*. 2 Vols. (Springfield, Mass.: G. Bill, 1863-66). For a similar later comment, see Lemuel L. Akin to Lossing, 11 February 1865, Alexander Brown Papers, College of William and Mary, Box 3, folder 51.

16. Childs to Lossing, 20 April 1863, LS 475, Lossing Addenda Box 9, Huntington Library; Childs to Lossing, 27 September 1864, Lossing Collection, Syracuse University Library, Box 1.

17. Childs to Lossing, 6 July 1863, Lossing Collection, Syracuse University Library, Box 1; Childs to Lossing, 30 March 1863, LS 474, Lossing Addenda Box 9, Lossing Collection, Huntington Library. The Charles Knight work was *The Popular History of England*. 8 Vols. (London: Bradbury and Evans, [1856-62?]). The first American edition was (Boston: Little, Brown, and Company, 1864).

18. "Authors At Home," *American Publishers' Circular* n.s. 1 (1 July 1863): 198. See also the same column earlier in that volume (1 May 1863): 5. Lossing to Mrs. Lossing, 7 July 1863, LS 1191, Lossing Addenda Box 9, Lossing Collection, Huntington Library; Lossing to Mrs. Lossing, 9 July 1863, LS 1193, Ibid.; LS 1134, Lossing's Notes from these and other travels, same collection.

19. On Fort Fisher, see Lossing to Mrs. Lossing, 27 December 1864, LS 1218, Lossing Addenda Box 10, Lossing Collection, Huntington Library, and LS 47 Book I, Lossing's journal of the siege, same collection. Also useful was Childs to Lossing, 22 December 1864, Call No. 9040, University of Virginia. In the late 1870s, Lossing wrote an account of the expedition for the *Philadelphia Times*; see Lossing, "The First Attack on Fort Fisher," *The Annals of the War* (reprint ed. Dayton, Ohio: Morningside House, Inc., 1988), pp. 228-40. Wallace to Grant, 8 December 1864, LS 1197, Lossing Addenda Box 10, Lossing Collection, Huntington Library. See also J. A. McAllister to Lossing, 14 January 1864, Lossing Papers, Syracuse University Library, Box 1; Lossing to Samuel Morse, 11 April 1864, Morse Manuscripts, Columbia University; Lossing to Wallace, 27 April 1864, Wallace Collection, Library of Congress.

20. Alex[.] Haight to Lossing, 8 April 1865, Lossing Collection, Hayes Library, Box 1. Kidder to Lossing, 10 April 1865, Ibid., Box 5; Lossing to Mrs. Lossing, 21 April 1865, LS 1228, Lossing Addenda Box 11, Lossing Collection, Huntington Library.

21. Childs to Lossing, 3 July 1865 and 6 July 1865, LS 489 and LS 490, respectively, Lossing Addenda Box 11, Lossing Collection, Ibid..

22. "Notes on Books and Booksellers," *American Literary Gazette and Publishers' Circular* n.s. 6 (1 January 1866): 154; "List of Books Recently Published in the United States," Ibid., n.s. 7 (15 June 1866): 88. On public impatience, see F. J. Dreer to Lossing, 27 January 1866, Lossing Collection, Hayes Library, Box 3.

23. Lieber to Lossing, 8 June 1866, LS 983, Lossing Addenda Box 12, Lossing Collection, Huntington Library; Milo P. Jewett to Lossing, 11 June 1866, Lossing Collection, Vassar College, Box 2. See also Samuel Y. Atlee to Lossing, 29 May 1866, Joseph J. Younglove to Lossing, 2 June 1866, and T. Cheney to Lossing, 20 September 1866, all in Lossing Collection, Syracuse University Library, Box 1.

24. New York *Herald*, 29 May 1866, quoted in "Notes on Books and Booksellers," *American Literary Gazette and Publishers' Circular* n.s. 7 (15 June 1866): 80; "Literary Notices," *Godey's* 73 (October 1866): 357. Another positive notice was "Literary," *Harper's Weekly* 10 (2 June 1866): 339. Childs reprinted this and other reviews; copies of these are in the Lossing Collection, Historical Society of Pennsylvania. See also "New Publications," Burlington, Vermont *Daily Free Press*, 29 May 1866, p. 2 col. 4.

25. On Lieber, see "Nationalism," *Harper's Weekly* 12 (18 April 1868): 243; Frank Friedel, *Francis Lieber: Nineteenth-Century Liberal* (Baton Rouge, La.: Louisiana State University Press, 1947); and David Herbert Donald, *Liberty and Union* (Lexington, Mass. and Toronto: D. C. Heath and Co., 1978), pp. 217-19, 223-24.

26. Lossing to Childs, 22 March 1866, Lossing Collection, Hayes Library, Box 1.

27. Lossing, *American Centenary* (Philadelphia: Porter & Coates, 1876), pp. 493-500. In 1879, Childs invited Lossing to a social function, and Lossing accepted. "Things in New York," *Philadelphia Public Ledger*, 3 February 1879, p. 1 col. 9.

28. Lossing to O. D. Case, 5 April 1867, LS 1274, Lossing Addenda Box 12, Lossing Collection, Huntington Library. Case's project was Horace Greeley's *American Conflict*; Case to Lossing, 11 April 1867, Lossing Collection, Syracuse University Library, Box 1.

29. Joseph Wilson, Jr. to Lossing, 28 May 1867, Lossing Papers, New York Public Library; J. L. Freeman to Lossing, 15 July 1867, LS 665, Lossing Addenda Box 12, Lossing Collection, Huntington Library.

30. *American Literary Gazette and Publishers' Circular* n.s. 10 (15 November 1867): 44.

31. Lossing to Duyckinck, 28 November 1867, Duyckinck-Halleck file, New York Public Library; Lossing to Alfred Day, 9 November 1867, Lossing Collection, Syracuse University Library, Box 3. Lossing Diary, 3 February 1868, LS 1137, Lossing Collection, Huntington Library.

32. Lossing, *The Pictorial Field-Book of the Civil War*. 3 Vols. (New York: T. Belknap, 1868-1869); later editions to 1881.

33. 22 April 1868 entry in Lossing Diary, LS 1137, Lossing Collection, Huntington Library; Belknap to Lossing, 23 December 1868, Lossing Collection, Hayes Library, Box 2; Lossing to Munsell, 26 January 1869, Lossing Collection, Syracuse University Library, Box 3.

34. John W. Draper, *History of the American Civil War*. 3 Vols. (New York: Harper & Brothers, 1867-1870); Horace Greeley, *The American Conflict: A History of the Great Rebellion.* 2 Vols. (Hartford, Conn.: O. D. Case & Company, 1864-1866). One review of Lossing's second volume did appear in *The Nation* 7 (16 July 1868): 55-56.

35. Among works in this genre, see John Smith Dye, *History of the Plots and Crimes of the Great Conspiracy to Overthrow Liberty in America* (New York: Published by the Author, 1866); J. Arthur Partridge, *The Making of the American Nation, or the Rise and Decline of Oligarchy in the West* (Philadelphia: J. B. Lippincott and Co., 1866); [Lewis H. Putnam], *Review of the Revolutionary Elements of the Rebellion* (Brooklyn: n.p., 1868); Henry Wilson, *History of the Rise and Fall of the Slave Power in America.* 3 Vols. (Boston: J. R. Osgood and Company, 1872-1877); John A. Logan, *The Great Conspiracy: Its Origin and History* (New York: A. R. Hart & Co., 1886).

36. Lossing Civil War manuscript, Part I, p. 14, Lossing Collection, Huntington Library.

37. Lossing to Rev. H. W. Bellows, 21 April 1862, Bellows Papers, Massachusetts Historical Society; see also Lossing to Francis Lieber, LI 2683, 22 August 1862, Lieber Collection, Huntington Library; Lossing to Henry O'Reilley, 31 October 1862, Item 1240-8, O'Reilley Collection, Rochester Public Library. For similar ideas, see George Duffield, Jr., *The God of Our Fathers: An Historical Sermon* (Philadelphia: Pugh, 1861); J. E. Caruthers, *God's Hand in the War* (Pittsburgh: Ferguson & Co., 1863). The best secondary source remains George Fredrickson, *The Inner Civil War: Northern Intellectuals and the Crisis of the Union* (New York: Harper & Row, 1965).

38. Lossing to John McAllister, 10 October 1862, Lossing Collection, Syracuse University Library, Box 3. Lossing to Henry O'Reilley, 29 December 1862, Item 1240-10, O'Reilley Collection, Rochester Public Library.

39. Lossing to Seward, 3 September 1863, Seward Papers, University of Rochester, enclosing copy of *Times* letter, from which I quoted.

40. Lossing to Johnson, 24 November 1864, reprinted in *The Papers of Andrew Johnson: Volume 7, 1864-1865*, ed. Leroy P. Graf [et. al.] (Knoxville, Tenn.: The University of Tennessee Press, 1986), pp. 313-14; quotation from p. 314. Lossing to Mrs. Lossing, 15 April 1865, LS 1226, Lossing Addenda Box 11, Lossing Collection, Huntington Library.

41. The *Pictorial History*'s third volume reflected the change in Lossing'41.22 attitude toward Johnson; compare p. 285n with pp. 613-14, 615.

42. Lossing to Beecher, 10 September 1866, Beecher Family Manuscripts, Yale University Library, Box 12, folder 480. Beecher's letter appeared with accompanying documents in "Reconstruction of the Southern States," in Beecher, *Patriotic Addresses*, ed. John R. Howard (New York: Fords, Howard, & Hulbert, 1891), pp. [736]-49. In a separate episode, Lossing saved a *New York Times* clipping (3 March 1868) about Beecher raising money for Robert E. Lee's college. Lossing comment on the clipping was that it represented "[a] most shameful endorsement of one of the most infamous men of the Rebellion." On the clipping's envelope, he wrote "Henry Ward Beecher's endorsement of Robert E. Lee [,] the Lucifer of the Rebellion[.]" Lossing Addenda Box 29, Lossing Collection, Huntington Library.

43. Lossing Diary, 6 January 1868, LS 1137, Same collection. See also 21 February, 26 February entries.

44. Lossing to Lieber, 1 October 1868, LI 2685, Lieber Collection, same repository.

8

WITH REDOUBLED EFFORTS: 1868–1880

After completing his *History of the Civil War*, Lossing remained busy with disparate projects. His most enduring effort in these years was the *Pictorial Field-Book of the War of 1812*. In content and style, the *Field-Book* contained much of Lossing's best work, and it remained a standard source on its topic for a century. Still, the volume never enjoyed the commercial favor Lossing wanted, so by the early 1870s, he continued to scramble for profitable endeavors, finally hitting upon Centennial literature as his flagging career's best hope.

To an even greater extent than in the 1850s, Lossing redoubled his already prodigious efforts to win public favor. In some cases, his works owed little to his undertakings as a pictorial historian. But at other times, his reputation as a recorder of historical sites was the basis for new ventures and revisions of old ones. This was true not only in his works' contents but in the publication and marketing strategies he used.

Significant along these lines was Lossing's continued interest in Washington's estate at Mount Vernon. As an earlier chapter noted, his book, *Mount Vernon and Its Associations*, reflected antebellum efforts to preserve the mansion and grounds. During the War, Lossing and publisher W. A. Townsend began planning a new edition. Even after its reappearance as *The Home of Washington* (1865), marketing presented challenges, as when Townsend had to remind Lossing that he had agreed to circulate the new edition by subscription rather than through bookstores. Townsend's hope in making this change was that he could "dispose of some 2 or 3 thousand a year instead of as many hundreds by booksellers."[1]

Through several editions of the book, Lossing's ties with the Mount Vernon Ladies' Association, the group that purchased and preserved the estate, deepened and took on new complexities. Sometimes his involvement in that group overlapped with his book's promotion, as when Lossing suggested the Association sell copies to visitors. At other times the question of sales seemed far from Lossing's mind or, more commonly, he sought to avoid any hint that he supported the Association out of selfish interests. As in so many aspects of his career, we cannot precisely weigh the significance of altruism and self-interest in these exertions. His efforts to help the Association often revealed a mixture of these concerns.

Lossing's involvement in the cause led to an extended correspondence with Pamela Ann Cunningham, the movement's prime actor. Earlier their relationship mostly involved exchanges of compliments. That element persisted, as Lossing continued to express high regard for Cunningham. He told one correspondent that "I believe her devotion to the cause to be as disinterested as the affection of a mother for her child[.]"[2]   Yet the connection was not without tensions, especially as Cunningham and Lossing tried to clarify Mount Vernon's standing in national culture.

When Cunningham wrote to Lossing, she typically concentrated on ideas for raising funds.[3]   Lossing did not ignore fiscal issues, but he took a distinct tack on them. He grew concerned that the Association might not be using its funds wisely, especially in buying relics to turn Mount Vernon into a museum. He tried to dissuade Cunningham from paying inflated prices for such items, arguing that once the Association secured funds its priorities should lay elsewhere. "I think that the first object to be obtained is an Endowment fund to beautify and preserve the mansion and grounds. When the public shall see that all is in good order and it shall be apparent that everything is well-managed, there will be a disposition among the owners of mementoes of Washington and his times to make the mansion the depository of many precious things."[4]

Meanwhile, Lossing finished his major work of this period: *The Pictorial Field-Book of the War of 1812.*[5]   Lossing had conducted research for this work since the 1850s, and earlier books included expressions of his interest. The *Field-Book of the Revolution* contained a score of references to "our last war with Great Britain." Lossing's most significant remark came at that work's conclusion, as he intimated that a favorable reception to the present work might induce him to compile another. "Should time deal gently with us, we may again go out with staff and scrip together upon the great highway of our country's progress, to note the march of events there. Until then, adieu!"[6]

In embarking on a history of the War of 1812, Lossing was entering an historiographical field that, while not as large as the Revolution or the Civil War, had produced many books and periodical essays. In 1815 and soon afterwards, the conflict inspired a spate of polemical histories.[7] Biographies of war heroes dominated the 1820s and the 1830s, although some political studies also appeared.[8]   In the late 1840s, public interest in the Mexican War spurred more works on the earlier conflict; those of Charles Ingersoll and John Jenkins were among the most notable.[9] The 1850s witnessed continued vitality in this literature, with Joel T. Headley, Charles Peterson, and others producing significant volumes.[10]

Lossing's work on the project continued through the 1850s, with veterans and others encouraging his efforts. In 1854, one contact offered to help Lossing when his research efforts brought him to the Upper South. He predicted the book "will *take*'—will sell most readily[.]"[11] Through 1860, research on the project dominated Lossing's time and energy, and offered motivation for his 1860-1861 travels in the Gulf Coast states as the Civil War began.

Once the Civil War ended, work on his history of that conflict did not prevent Lossing from pushing ahead with the other project. Late in 1866, Harper & Brothers were almost ready to put the book in type; then suddenly, apparently due to delays in writing, the project stalled. By April 1868, one contact finally exhausted his patience and blurted out to a third party "[i]s friend Lossing waiting for all the *Veterans* of *1812* [sic] to die off before he publishes his pictorial history?" This query found its answer within three weeks, as Lossing sent the book's conclusion to Harpers. "I feel grateful to Almighty God for the preservation of my health and life," he wrote in his diary, "to finish this work of nearly 1100 pages, and illustrated by about 900 engravings[.]"[12]

Lossing's task in the new *Field-Book* was daunting because he covered not only the second Anglo-American war but the diplomatic and political events that preceded it. Lossing's concern to begin with the 1783 Treaty of Paris and so connect the book with the Revolution required preliminary reflections on the American Revolution's character. Lossing did not deny that, in one sense, the patriots were rebels. But "[t]heir rebellion instantly assumed the dignity of a revolution, and commanded the respect and sympathy of the civilized nations" (17). This expressed Lossing's inconsistent but wide-ranging views on revolutions as positive or negative focal points of historical change. This theme reappeared under various guises in the new volume.

Despite the Revolution's achievements, Lossing depicted the years immediately after 1783 as a period of economic, political, and social chaos in the new nation. The nationalistic solution of a Federal Constitution, although earning Lossing's applause, received scant treatment. Lossing offered no details on the Philadelphia convention that drafted the Constitution or on the Bill of Rights, but he did observe that through the amended Constitution the United States "became absolutely independent[.]" For Lossing, later national history, especially through 1815, represented a process of political leaders elucidating and solidifying the Constitution's achievement (35 [quotation], 116).

Later chapters emphasized that process's overlapping political and diplomatic aspects. Lossing's discussion of American diplomacy through the 1790s required some comments on that "moral earthquake": the French Revolution.[13]   This gave him the opportunity to contrast a negative European upheaval with America's good revolutionary heritage. Lossing wrote in positive terms of the French Revolution's early, moderate phase in which Lafayette played a role. "The good and the brave of the kingdom had long perceived the abyss of woe upon the brink of which their country was poised, and with a heroism which in the light of history appears almost divine, they resolved to sound the trumpet of political reform, and arouse king, nobles, and people to a sense of solemn duty as men and patriots." (60).

The Reign of Terror in which the "ferocious" Jacobins murdered thousands "revealed to the people of the United States those terrible aspects of the French Revolution which made them for a moment recoil in horror" and realize the justice of Federalists' fears. When the National Assembly took control of the government from Lafayette and joined "the mad populace" in demanding the king's overthrow, "Paris was drunk with passion and unrestrained license." The Jacobin "conspirators" then "took bolder steps" by abolishing the monarchy, creating a republic in its stead, and declaring war on neighboring monarchies. When the insanity climaxed with Louis's execution, "the civilized world looked upon the sanguinary tragedy on the Gallic stage with dismay and horror" (74-75, 76).

Lossing relished these details for their indirect utility in attacking Jeffersonian Republicanism. He recounted the Republicans' dinners celebrating the French monarch's death and the French Republic's conquest of the Austrian Netherlands. Such tasteless displays demonstrated that Jefferson and his followers "were blind to the total difference between their own Revolution and that in France" and "forgetful of the Friendship of Holland during [the Revolutionary War]" (77). Lossing was concerned that readers not mistake French rhetoric about "liberty, equality, and fraternity" with the truly noble values of 1776. Political and historical perspectives converged when he attributed the confusion to the Jeffersonian Democratic Societies' propaganda. "These societies and the newspapers in their interest attempted to deceive the people by comparing the French Revolution to their own, as equally justified and holy. Many, totally uninformed of the facts, believed; but enlightenment and better counsels kept their passions in check. The informed and thoughtful saw no just comparison between the two Revolutions" (81n).

As Lossing analyzed foreign affairs, he concluded that both England and France were "unscrupulous . . . powers" deserving censure for their "desperate game" of violating American neutral rights. This depiction of pre-war foreign affairs gave Lossing an opportunity to trace the war's causes. On this score, he devoted nearly all his attention to the British impressment of American sailors, a "nefarious practice" that compromised national independence. He also cited the British prohibition on American trade with

France as a significant issue, but maintained that impressment was far more crucial (145, 147, 153, 186, 212, 247, 248, 455n, 468).

Lossing's conclusion reiterated that the war's significance lay in securing "the positive and permanent independence of the United States, and with it a guarantee to the posterities, of the perpetuation and growth of free institutions." The outcome of the Civil War, he continued, made the nation's survival yet more certain. Thus in his broader view of American history, the War of 1812 stood at once as heir to the Revolution and precursor to the Civil War, and therefore a necessary facet of national evolution (1067 [quotation], 1069).

Since Lossing devoted hundreds of pages to the Second Anglo-American war's military aspects, he inevitably had many chances to depict the competence and moral standing of various combatants. Although his treatment of American forces tended toward favoritism and their British and Amerindian foes usually appeared in a worse light, specific instances varied widely.

In earlier chapters, Lossing pilloried Great Britain for inciting Native Americans against the United States and for refusing to negotiate trade and impressment issues. Later he gave almost no attention to such policies, concentrating instead on the good or bad character of individual commanders. The gallant General Issac Brock stood in sharp contrast to Colonel Henry Proctor, who Lossing described as a boastful, cruel coward. Elsewhere Lossing did not hesitate to remark that certain British officers were "most faithful and active" in performing their duties, often "under the impulses of the purest patriotism only" (357, 387-88, 395n, 440n).

Some of Lossing's strongest language appeared as he described the Amerindians who fought on the British side. These were "savages" on a "bloody errand[,]" "bands of murderers and miscreants[,]" a "motley foe" of "red blood-hounds", "like fierce and famished tigers . . . hideously painted . . . a host devilish in appearance, and on a demoniac errand." They confronted an American force "with vigilant eyes and malignant hearts" and became "excited by the shedding of blood" (256, 344, 358, 408n, 488, 533, 753-54). Lossing sometimes suggested that the "savages" were more stupid than evil, since the British so easily manipulated them. Occasionally, he intimated that white settlers caused problems that led to war, and that a primitive patriotism and love of liberty motivated the best Native American leaders—Joseph Brant, Tecumtha (Lossing's spelling) and Weatherford (45-46, 187-88, 355, 422, 746, 754, 756).

In contrast to his characterizations of British and Native Americans, Lossing wrote many favorable things about American military leaders, common soldiers, and sailors. Many "forgotten" American heroes won inclusion in Lossing's pantheon through the footnote-style biographical sketches that littered his text. As in the *Field-Book of the Revolution*, these capsule biographies not only recorded information but hopefully made the volume more appealing to readers. Lossing sat few limits on the praise he gave to patriotic individuals in these sketches. His favorite summary remark was to write that these men or women were "useful" in safeguarding the American cause. Much of Lossing's concern for celebrating "useful" patriots' lives was to remind Americans that they should preserve and respect their gravesites or other memorials. Fears that America might imitate past republics in lacking gratitude for heroes prompted him to lament the ruin of General Pike's burial site (616-17).

Lossing did not limit discussion to events long past; rather, he used interpretations of history to develop nationalistic perspectives on recent developments—especially the sectional conflict and the Civil War. The culmination of the sectional crisis during the time Lossing researched and wrote the *Field-Book* kept the memories of southern treason close to his mind.

Direct or implied attacks on southern secession and the state-rights ideology that sustained it appeared throughout the *Field-Book*. A treatment of pre-Constitutional politics gave Lossing an opportunity to criticize the Articles of Confederation as embodying these ideas. Nationalists like Alexander Hamilton who perceived the Confederation's fatal weaknesses "foresaw the dangers of the doctrine of supreme state sovereignty, which has wrought so much mischief in our day." State-rights ideologues opposed the Constitution, but the public's wisdom insured ratification (26n).

Such comments did not draw comment from Lossing's correspondents or some published reviews, although for others they proved crucial. Letters from antiquarians about the new *Field-Book* were almost universally enthusiastic. Henry Onderdonk, Jr., a historian from Long Island, decided that "I must call it your masterpiece[.]" Lawyer-historian Brantz Mayer claimed to speak for other readers in Baltimore when he remarked that "[w]e are to be greatly your debtors for the record of the war of 1812." Mayer lauded the work's clarity and felicity of style. "I have been reading your book and am very much pleased with the manner in which you have considered, in admirable style, the vast mass of materials and events. I have been particularly struck by the force and lucidity with which you state the history of our troubles during the Confederacy[.]"[14]

Most periodical notices of the *Field-Book* took a friendly tack. Predictably, *Harper's Weekly* printed a favorable review, contending that along with the *Field-Book of the Revolution*, Lossing's new volume was "indispensable to every library." A Philadelphia *Press* reviewer thought the book much better than Lossing's history of the Civil War. Further, that writer noted, the new work's strict chronological treatment gave it advantages over the *Field-Book of the Revolution*. A religious journal had an equally laudatory response, calling the *Field-Book* "[o]ne of the attractive books of the Lossing series, for long years familiar to American households."[15]

Other reviews displayed negative perspectives, and Lossing's comments on the Civil War often inspired these. A Democratic magazine, *The Old Guard*, offered a caustic notice that stressed the irony of Lossing's earlier success in celebrating "our rebel fathers" of the Revolution. Regarding the new *Field-Book*, the reviewer complained that it "abounds with stump-speech eloquence, and the politics of the bar-room brawler[.]" Lossing "loses no opportunity to step aside from the current of his narrative, in order to assail the carcase [sic] of the Southern 'rebellion,' and hesitates at no absurdities of expression in order to gratify malice, or possibly to pander to a sectional hate which he has not the sagacity to see is dying out before the pecuniary difficulties of the time, and the force of reason." In this way, the work "shows the narrow mind and thorough incapacity of Mr. Lossing."[16]

The sharpest criticism came from Henry B. Dawson, antiquarian and editor of the *Historical Magazine*. This notice, the most critical that any of Lossing's books received, started with a back-handed compliment to the *Field-Book of the Revolution*. The earlier work's travelogue construction possessed sufficient novelty to attract many readers for whom conventional history held no interest. "The *Field-book* before us, however, is nearly a complete abandonment of this new process; and it restores the ordinary chronological arrangement of the narrative to the position from which the former *Field-book* so agreeably hurled it[.]"

Dawson's criticisms all dealt with the *Field-Book*'s first chapter and emphasized that Lossing "too often sacrifices his fidelity as a historian for the sake of rhetorical effect." Dawson satirized Lossing's adoration for John Jay and Alexander Hamilton. He challenged Lossing's repetition of "the oft-told balderdash concerning the apocryphal Confederation," arguing that foreign nations respected the United States during the Confederation and that domestic unrest was no more prevalent before 1787 than later.

As his attack progressed, Dawson reemphasized Lossing's ignorance or willful distortion of sources on the Confederation. "It is well, sometimes, to be quite sure of the value of one's authorities before undertaking to write *history*; when writing *romance* one needs take less trouble." Dawson's political sympathies grew evident as he argued that Lossing's "pen was stayed in its holy work of bearing testimony to the Truth, because of the injury which it might do to the temper or the reputation of a dominant political party." Dawson concluded "that Mr. Lossing has examined the authorities only for the establishment of a preconceived theory, . . . for the support . . . of a controlling political party, and in defiance of the authorities on which historians delight to lean: in sad disregard, too, of his reputation as a faithful historian."[17]

The *Historical Magazine* review apparently had little impact on the *Field-Book*'s commercial fortunes, because long before that article appeared sales had disappointed Lossing and his publisher. At first, Harper & Brothers felt confident of success. John W. Harper, Jr., noting Lossing's birthday in

February 1868, projected that in another year the firm might sell 10,000 copies. Rather than high sales, that year brought revisions in royalty agreements and, in June 1869, an admission that the book had failed on the subscription market. As was common for this era, precise sales figures have not survived. But Lossing soon decided that the *Field-Book* would not do well, so he forfeited all rights to the work in return for $6,500 from Harpers.[18]

Lossing's manuscripts from these years do not reveal whether the work's slow sales troubled him. Whatever his state of mind, Lossing somehow maintained his frenzied pace of writing, although his focus shifted. As the mid-1870s loomed, anticipations of the 1876 Centennial of American Independence spurred him to quickly write still more books. In the process he sought to exploit the public interest that he anticipated and tried to channel. As in earlier episodes, the results did not always match his plans.

For nineteenth-century Americans, historical consciousness climaxed in 1876 with local and national celebrations of the Centennial of national independence. Philadelphia's Exposition offered a major example of such commemorations. That event's emphasis on contemporary technology over historical recreations did not diminish awareness of some milestones the country had now reached; indeed, it glorified present-day technical prowess as proving that Americans had, in some ways if not others, realized their Revolution's promise. This proved a central theme for Lossing's major commemorative book, *American Centenary*.

As Lossing prepared for the Centennial, one event revealed his high standing among some academic scholars: the University of Michigan granted him an honorary Doctorate of Laws (LL.D.) degree. This came about because Lossing had developed a friendship with Moses Coit Tyler, a Poughkeepsie native then teaching history at Michigan. Tyler later moved back to New York, worked at Cornell, and proved an important scholar of the Revolutionary War.[19] Acting at Tyler's urging, Michigan's Regents granted Lossing the degree in June 1872, although they formally bestowed it the next year.[20]

Lossing's first effort for the Centennial market was *Our Country*, a multi-volume survey of national history that Johnson & Miles of New York published while Centennial interest was at its height. Lossing's note on the final manuscript summarized much about the work's production and publication history. "For the preparation of this work . . . I received $4 a printed page. . . . The work (First Edition) was completed in the Spring of 1877; the enlarged 2d [sic] Edition was completed in the autumn of 1877."[21] At this rate Lossing must have received about $6,400 for the 1,600-page survey, perhaps more for the later edition.

Our Country broke with most of Lossing's earlier works when he took no responsibility for its illustrations. Felix O. C. Darley, a Philadelphia native then famous for book and magazine engravings, prepared over 500 pictures that appeared as both line drawings and inset plates. From the project's inception, the publisher expressed a desire "that both Author and Artist will work harmoniously and effectively together." So far as satisfaction with Darley's work was concerned, Lossing realized these hopes, finding the pictures "very spirited."[22] When *Our Country* appeared, Lossing maintained that Darley's illustrations should prove "positively useful, not only as artistic embellishments, but as safe instructors" (I: vii).

Johnson & Miles promoted the Lossing-Darley collaboration, and the public response rewarded their efforts. In late 1876, Lossing reported that between 40,000 and 50,000 subscriptions were already in place, although actual publication was still almost a year away. Six months later he exalted in *Our Country*'s "extraordinary sale," considering negative economic conditions. By September 1877, the figure passed 50,000, which Lossing again called "extraordinary[.]" Finally, in March 1878, Lossing revealed that Johnson & Miles had printed over 70,000 copies, apparently knowing they could dispose of them.[23] These results held some irony, since Lossing wrote the volumes for a flat fee and realized no benefit from high sales.

Similar arrangements held for another Centennial work that did not enjoy *Our Country*'s popularity: *American Centenary*, a bulky one-volume survey of technical, social, and intellectual progress that Porter & Coates of Philadelphia published. In early 1875, that firm approached Lossing about writing such a book and initially met resistance. Later Porter & Coates tried to convince Lossing that he should undertake the project. Playing their trump-card at the start, they mentioned "that there is *every* probability that the volume will be published as officially sanctioned by [the Philadelphia Exposition's] Centennial Board of Finance, they deriving some revenue from its sale." They thought, correctly, that official connections would impress Lossing. Soon he agreed to write the book for $2,700.[24]

Through 1875, Lossing conducted research for the *Centenary*. He solicited data from antiquarians throughout the country.[25] Lossing also gathered information from factory owners, planning to make celebratory histories of firms and executives an attraction of the book. In May 1876, his publishers bluntly criticized Lossing for relying too much on these sources, especially in the biographical sketches Lossing wanted in *Centenary*. "[A]lthough we want all the parties to be satisfied with the matter relating to them in the work, yet we have not bound ourselves nor have we expected *you* to write just what they want said about themselves at their dictation."[26]

With his task nearly done, Lossing reflected on the Centennial's larger meaning. He encouraged one correspondent's interest in American history as appropriate to the year's celebrations. "It always gives me pleasure when I hear of a young businessman cultivating a taste for the historical literature of our country—a literature as full of romance and dramatic interest as the best-dressed work of fiction. And I think every American citizen is justified in feeling a pride in being called an *American citizen*, when we glance over the history of our Republic during the first one hundred years of its existence."[27] Both *Our Country* and *American Centenary* buttressed these comfortable perspectives on the nation's past, present, and future.

The United States as the apex of progress was a major theme in *Our Country*. For Lossing, America's redemptive function was already operative during European exploration. "When at near the close of the fifteenth century Columbus crossed the Atlantic, the faint gleam was seen of the dawn of that glorious day in the history of civilization, whose sunrise was heralded by the bold assertion that man had an inalienable right to the free exercise of his reason in faith and practice, whether in religion, politics, or morality" (I: 32).

American history as the story of emergent liberty remained Lossing's central motif in Volume Three. The sectional crisis and Civil War dominated Lossing's final volume, largely because he thought that a slave-power conspiracy against the government had been operative over several decades. When Lossing surveyed the war itself, his comments typically duplicated his *Pictorial History* of that conflict. As in the *History*, Lossing castigated Robert E. Lee's desertion from the Federal ranks, and labeled the Confederacy as a pseudo-government (III: 1383, 1405, 1411, 1413, 1432). But one element in his interpretation of the sectional conflict was new.

That fresh perspective appeared when Lossing began writing about the Civil War and the Black Emancipation it brought as representing a positive "social revolution." This was significant because in earlier writings (and even later ones) Lossing could never bring himself to label laudable social or political movements as "revolutions"; indeed he typically was more concerned that they be devoid of revolutionary content due to his conservative political and social convictions. But in *Our Country*, Lossing's argument was that the recent "social revolution" had fulfilled an earlier Revolution's promise, and hence insured the American experiment's success (III: [1395], 1692).

American Centenary was nearly as optimistic as *Our Country* and less complex in its structure. Its historical passages mostly reiterated arguments from other works. Lossing asserted again that the American Revolution was conservative.

The colonists were not revolutionists. They fought not to acquire liberty, for that they already possessed by prescriptive right. They struggled to defend their natural and chartered liberties, and the rights asserted at Runnymede five hundred years before, and which every British subject claimed to be his lawful treasure. . . . The king and the parliament were the aggressors. They were the revolutionists. The colonists waited patiently for justice and reconciliation, until there was no longer a shadow of hope for either (3,4).

On the post-Revolution years, Lossing made conventional statements on the Confederation's inadequacies and the Constitution's virtues (3, 4, 7, 347).

Many passages offered perspectives on the role of commerce and industry in national progress.   Lossing gave trade a key place in American development, contending that material and spiritual prosperity had grown together. His survey of American commercial activity climaxed in praise for national progress.

In every department of work we have realized . . . the wildest dreams of our youth, as a nation. We have established a sound, graceful and attractive political structure; . . . a healthful social system . . . we have set the candles of popular education on every hill . . . we have spread the light of civilization and Christianity over a continent. . . . And all this is the result of less than one hundred years of progress (325).

Lossing discussed various social issues that cheered or discouraged him. The problem that most riveted his attention involved Native Americans' place in the national order. Lossing viewed Amerindians as impediments to national progress, but he blamed that on whites' mistreatment of them. "Athwart the pathways of civilization in its westward march, stand the hostile remnants of savage tribes, . . . who have been made restless, dissatisfied, suspicious, and revengeful, by the results of unwise statesmanship, and of positive wrong-doing toward them." He criticized the nation's early leaders for misjudging the Native Americans' character. "Had the founders of the Republic looked upon the Indian as a man as susceptible of cultivation as the savage Britons from whom many of them were descended, and made the barbarian a citizen, . . . great wrongs, great distresses, and great scandals might have been avoided" (398).

In his conclusion, Lossing reasserted that recent events made certain not just the nation's survival but its triumph. "The result of the late Civil War, . . . satisfied the American people that the republican form of government, properly administered, and our Republic itself were not, any longer, subjects of 'mere experiments,' as monarchists had long persistently asserted, but that ample demonstration had been given of the power of republicanism resting upon patriotism and virtue, and of the Republic of the West" ([579]). But as this discussion has shown, Lossing's sanguine perspective had limits. Problems in the treatment of Native Americans especially troubled him and forced him to recognize that reality should come nearer to the ideals Americans held.

On a fiscal level as well, Lossing's hopes did not always mesh with experience. Except for *Our Country,* his books from the mid-1870s, despite the immense labor they involved, did not prove commercially successful. As in other episodes in Lossing's career, we know little about why this happened. *American Centenary* was a physically imposing volume with steel engravings that made it too expensive for many readers. Besides, Lossing had attained fame as a historical writer, and little of *American Centenary* offered any connected narrative of past events such as people expected from him.

Consequently, Lossing's search for profitable ventures persisted past

1880, as, now almost seventy years old, he entered his life's final decade. This period brought some successful works, and even set-backs did not threaten Lossing's middle-class standing. But some of his late failures damaged his relationship with specific publishers, especially the firm that had issued his most important books: Harper & Brothers. When that fissure developed, Lossing again felt pressed to employ ingenuity in preserving his career.

NOTES

1. Townsend to Lossing, 28 March 1867, Lossing Collection, Hayes Library, Box 8.

2. Lossing to Mrs. Halsted, 2 April 1870. I saw two copies of this letter: one as LS 1294 in Lossing Addenda Box 14, Lossing Collection, Huntington Library, the other in the Early Records of the Mount Vernon Ladies' Association, Mount Vernon Library.

3. Cunningham to Lossing, 8 March 1870, LS 538, Lossing Addenda Box 14, Lossing Collection, Huntington Library.

4. Lossing to Cunningham, 20 March 1870, Early Records of the Mount Vernon Ladies' Association, Mount Vernon Library.

5. Lossing, *The Pictorial Field-Book of the War of 1812* (New York: Harper & Brothers, 1868).

6. Lossing, *Field-Book of the Revolution*. 2 Vols. (New York: Harper and Brothers, 1855), I: p. 210; see also Ibid., I: pp. 139, 143, 166, 213, 220-21, 226, 613, 617-18, 628n, 635-36n, 675n, 699n; II: pp. 182-83n, 289n, 326, 326n, 426n, 427n, 434n, 552n, 554n, 644n. The final long quotation was from Ibid., II: p. 636.

7. Examples included: William Cobbett, *The Pride of Britannia Humbled* (New York: T. Boyle [et. al.], 1815); Samuel R. Brown, *An Authentic History of the Second War for Independence* (Auburn, N.Y.: J. G. Hathaway, Kellogg & Beardslee, 1815); John Lathrop, *A Compendious History of the Late War* (Boston: J. W. Burditt, 1815); T[homas] O'Connor, *An Impartial and Correct History of the War* (New York: J. Low, 1815); [Henry M. Brackenridge], *History of the Late War* (Baltimore: Joseph Cushing, 1816) and later editions to 1854.

8. John M. Niles, *The Life of Oliver Hazard Perry*. 2d Ed. (Hartford, Conn.: Oliver D. Cooke, 1821); S. Putnam Waldo, *The Life and Character of Stephen Decatur* (Middletown, Conn.: Clark & Lyman, 1821); Paris M. Davis, *An Authentick [sic] History of the Late War* (Ithaca, N.Y.: Davis & Saunders, 1829); [Abel Bowen], *The Naval Monument* (Boston: George Clark, 1830); Theodore Dwight, *History of the Hartford Convention* (New-York: N. & J. White; Boston: Russell, Odiorne, & Co., 1833); R. Thomas, *The Glory of America* (New York: E. Strong, 1835); Thomas Harris, *The Life and Services of Commodore William Bainbridge* (Philadelphia: Carey Lea & Blanchard, 1837); Tristam Burges, *Battle of Lake Erie* (Boston: B. B. Mussey, 1839).

9. Charles J. Ingersoll, *Historical Sketch of the Second War Between The United States of America, and Great Britain* (Philadelphia: Lea and Blanchard, 1849); John S. Jenkins, *The Generals of the Late War with Great Britain* (Auburn, N.Y.: Derby, Miller

& Co.; Buffalo: G. H. Derby & Co., 1849).

10. J. T. Headley, *The Second War with England*. 2 Vols. (New York: C. Scribner, 1853); Charles J. Peterson, *The Military Heroes of the War of 1812.* 10th Ed. (Philadelphia: Jas. B. Smith & Co., 1854).

11. A. W. Putnam to Draper, 4 May 1854, Series DD, vol. 15, p. 41, Draper Collection, State Historical Society of Wisconsin.

12. Dreer to Lossing, 1 July 1866, Lossing Collection, Hayes Library, Box 3; Howard Edwards to Lossing, 27 July 1866, Lossing Collection, Historical Society of Pennsylvania. Lossing to C. C. Burr, 12 September 1866, Clifton Waller Barrett Library: Lossing Section, University of Virginia; Stephen Champlin to Lossing, 17 December 1866, LS 455, Lossing Addenda Box 12, Lossing Collection, Huntington Library. C.S. Todd to Lyman C. Draper, 13 April 1868, Series U., Vol. 8, p. 22, Draper Collection. Lossing Diary, 6 May 1868, LS 1137, Lossing Collection, Huntington Library. See also Lossing to George Bancroft, 9 June 1868, Bancroft Papers, Massachusetts Historical Society, Lossing to Francis Lieber, 3 October 1868, LI 2687, Lieber Collection, Huntington Library.

13. Page 60. The same phrase appeared in John S. C. Abbott, *Lives of the Presidents of the United States of America* (Boston: B. B. Russell & Co., 1868), p. 91.

14. Onderdonk to Lossing, n.d. [1868?] and 27 January 1868, both in Lossing Collection, Hayes Library, Box 6; Mayer to Lossing, 28 April 1869, Lossing Collection, Syracuse University Library, Box 1; Mayer to Lossing, 23 August 1869, LS 1599, Lossing Addenda Box 13, Lossing Collection, Huntington Library.

15. "Notes," *Harper's Weekly* 13 (18 September 1869): 595; Philadelphia *Press* review described in R. S. MacKenzie to unidentified [not Lossing], 6 August 1869, LS 1580, Lossing Addenda Box 13, Lossing Collection, Huntington Library; this may be the same review in Lossing Addenda Box 29, Ibid.; "Book Notices," *New England Historic-Genealogical Register* 23 (October 1869): 483-84; "Editor's Book Table," *Harper's* 38 (March 1869): 561.

16. "Our Book Table," *The Old Guard* 7 (July 1869): [553]-54; *The Old Guard* 7 (September 1869): 714-15; quotation from p. 715.

17. [Dawson], "Trade Publications," *Historical Magazine* 17 [n.s. 7] (January 1870): 69-75.

18. J. W. Harper, Jr. to Lossing, 14 February 1868, LS 804, Lossing Addenda Box 13, Lossing Collection, Huntington Library. Sources on later decisions included three documents in the Harpers Archives, Reel 1: Contract Books Vol. 2: Memorandum of Agreement, 30 January 1869 (pp. A2 26-27); Lossing to Harper & Brothers, 29 June 1869 (p. A2 40); Indenture, 14 April 1873 (pp. A2 203-4).

19. On Tyler, see Alexander Moore's article in *American Historians, 1866-1912*, ed. Clyde N. Wilson, Vol. 47 of *Dictionary of Literary Biography* (Detroit: Gale Research Company, 1986), pp. 317-25; Michael Kammen, "Moses Coit Tyler: The First Professor of American History in the United States," in *Selvages & Biases: The Fabric of History in American Culture* (Ithaca, N.Y., and London: Cornell University Press, 1987), pp. 222-51.

20. Lossing to Angell, 17 May 1873, Angell Papers, University of Michigan, Box 1. Personal research and the kind help of archivists at the University of Michigan have not yielded clear evidence on the Regents' thinking in this matter. *Proceedings of the Board of Regents of the University of Michigan from January, 1870, to January, 1876* (Ann Arbor, Mich.: Courier Steam Printing House, 1876), p. 235, gave no hint of

motivations. See also Tyler telegraph to Lossing, 25 June 1872, Lossing Collection, Vassar College, Box 6; Tyler to Lossing, 27 June 1872, Lossing Collection, Syracuse University Library, Box 4 (a copy of a document at Vassar).

21. Lossing, *Our Country. A Household History for all Readers, from the Discovery of America to the One Hundredth Anniversary of the Declaration of Independence.* 3 Vols. (New York: Johnson & Miles, 1875-78) and many other editions dating to 1913. Two-volume editions exist; I own a three-volume edition and quote from it here. Undated Lossing note with LS 1 & 2, Lossing Collection, Huntington Library. Other manuscripts on *Our Country* include: Johnson, Wilson & Co. [earlier name of firm] to Lossing, 26 August 1873, 11 October 1873, 1 December 1874, all in Lossing Collection, Hayes Library Box 5; Lossing to Edwin Greble, 19 March 1877, Greble Papers, Library of Congress; Lossing to J. C. Buttre, 29 October 1877, Lossing Collection, Syracuse University Library, Box 3.

22. Johnson, Wilson & Co. to Lossing, 31 December 1873, and Gouv. Kemble to Lossing, 2 April 1875, both in Lossing Collection, Hayes Library, Box 5; Lossing to Evert A. Duyckinck, 15 March 1874, Duyckinck Collection, New York Public Library; Henry J. Johnson to Lossing, 22 June 1876, LS 918, Lossing Addenda Box 18, Lossing Collection, Huntington Library.

23. Lossing to S. W. Francis, M.D., 7 December 1876, Lossing Collection, Syracuse University Library, Box 3; Lossing to Evert A. Duyckinck, 15 June 1877, Duyckinck Collection, New York Public Library; Lossing to J. C. Buttre, 27 September 1877, manuscript description in Catalogue # 14, p. 16, Hudson Rogue Co., Nelsonville, New York; Lossing to Henry B. Carrington, 22 March 1878, Carrington Manuscripts, Yale University Library, Ms. 130, Box 3, Folder 43.

24. Lossing, *The American Centenary: A History of the Progress of the Republic of the United States during the First One Hundred Years of Its Existence* (Philadelphia: Porter & Coates, 1876). Porter & Coates to Lossing, 15 March 1875, Lossing Collection, Hayes Library, Box 7; Porter & Coates to Lossing, 25 March 1875, Ibid., Box 1. Porter & Coates was also the publisher of many of Horatio Alger's novels. See the article by Anna Lou Ashby in *Publishers for Mass Entertainment in Nineteenth [-] Century America*, ed. Madeleine B. Stern (Boston: G. K. Hall & Co., 1980), pp. 245-49.

25. Lossing to John B. Linn, 4 January 1875, Lossing Collection, Hayes Library, Box 1; Dreer to Lossing, 26 July 1875, Ibid., Box 3; A. T. Goshum to Lossing, 2 March 1875, Lossing Collection, Syracuse University Library, Box 2; Frank M. String to Lossing, 25 October 1875, LS 1855, Lossing Addenda Box 17, Lossing Collection, Huntington Library; Ch. Buckingham to Lossing, 7 January 1876, Lossing Collection, Adriance Memorial Library, Poughkeepsie.

26. Porter & Coates to Lossing, 27 May 1876, Lossing Collection, Historical Society of Pennsylvania. See also Lossing to Col. Richard M. Hoe, 28 July 1875, How Manuscripts, Columbia University.

27. Lossing to E. Stuckland, Jr., 13 May 1876, How Manuscripts, Columbia University.

9

DECLINE AND FALL:
1881–1891

By 1880, Lossing had accumulated half a century's experience in historical writing. He was nearing his seventieth birthday, and a cession of his endless work might have seemed proper. But Lossing continued writing at a hectic pace, as he repeated themes and topics from earlier works and attempted new approaches.

The new decade marked the fortieth anniversary of Lossing's involvement with Harper & Brothers, the New York publishers who had issued most of his important books. That connection began with the *Outline History of the Fine Arts* and blossomed in the Revolutionary and War of 1812 *Field-Books*. Starting in the late 1870s, Lossing and the firm made several efforts to realize new profits from their tie. These started hopefully, but soon faltered when some disastrous projects effectively ended the connection.

One project for Harper & Brothers proved ambitious but flawed: *Harpers' Popular Cyclopaedia of United States History* (1881) that went through a few editions during Lossing's life. In a vastly expanded form, Harpers reissued it into the twentieth century.To recall the *Southern Literary Messenger*'s categories from Chapter 1, nineteenth-century American writers often moved quickly between scholarly attainment and "scribbler" status. This was true for Lossing, who, through the 1850s, sought to further his career through many projects. A focus for this period was in biography, which Lossing viewed as a source for history's moral teachings. Some of his biographical works from these years proved memorable for contemporary readers. *Our Countrymen*, a volume of brief articles on significant Americans, impressed one antiquarian as "worth a dozen Plutarchs" in its potential for instructing youth.[1] Lossing and the publishers agreed to proceed with this work in 1878, and he concentrated on it for three years.[2]

In February 1881, John W. Harper wrote Lossing a detailed letter, trying to correct what he saw as Lossing's misapprehensions about the project. Harper said he was unsure whether to sell the work via subscription or the regular book trade and thought that he might try both. He said Lossing was wrong to assume subscription sales were necessarily higher, especially since business conditions seemed on the mend. Harper suggested the *Cyclopedia* should "have a genteel appearance to commend it to book-lovers, historical students & librarians instead of the vulgar, *bulky* look of the average subscription book sold by imprudence, importunity and persecution." He estimated that he might lose $20,000 if he could not sell 5,000 copies.[3]

With such fears serving as negative incentive, Lossing finished the *Cyclopedia*; late in 1881, the first edition appeared. In 1882, Harpers prepared an elaborate circular for subscription agents. It stressed Lossing's special fitness for the work, especially his visits to historical sites and skill as an illustrator. "In this way the author has done for American history what no other man has done or can do. His work as an artist is essentially the *Object-teaching of History*." The paper encouraged agents to memorize lists of topics that, the publishers hoped, would hold special appeal for "Public Men" or general readers. "Take the subjects you are most familiar with from these lists and learn them first. Be ready to turn to them when showing the book and recite the prominent features." The instructions stressed particular classes of customers as most vital to sales. "*There is no book so needed by public men. Their subscriptions must be first obtained; success is then sure to follow.*"[4]

But success proved elusive after the *Cyclopedia* appeared to mixed reviews. Not surprisingly, *Harper's Weekly* offered a glowing notice, arguing that the work's organization made it "convenient." But the New York *Tribune* expressed more critical thoughts. Its review depicted Lossing's new work as "singularly defective . . . [in] the distribution of his materials. He seems to have very little conception of the fundamental rule in alphabetical arrangements, that a title must be entered under its most important or most easily remembered word; and he has placed a great many of his articles where no one would think of looking for them."[5]

A Philadelphia paper admitted that the *Cyclopaedia* contained insightful writing, but also criticized its poor organization.

Some of the articles, we gladly say, are up to what we would expect from Dr. Lossing and are excellently done. . . . We must confess, however, that, judging from the whole, we do not think that Dr. Lossing was the man for the work. The school in which he has been educated did not fit him for it. He has been in the habit of treating subjects of wide scope, and has done so with ability. His pages of easy-flowing language, full of sunny pictures, have gained for him more real friends than any writer of American history, save Washington Irving. Many we know who love him through his books, and to them it will be, as it is to us, a disappointment, that this, which should be an epitome of his life-work, should be so deficient, both in symmetry and system.[6]

Even sharper rebukes came from William F. Poole, a librarian and historian. Poole echoed others in criticizing the entries' arrangement. But he expended more energy in attacking Lossing's uncritical mental habits, especially his propensity for accepting "exploded myth" as historical fact. This went against recent historiographical trends that Poole considered positive. "[Lossing's] reading in the later results of historical criticism appears, in the work before us, to be much narrower than we had supposed. It is enough for his purpose . . . that a narrative be picturesque and have some authority behind it."[7]

If the *Cyclopaedia of United States History* suffered from defective organization and poor reviews, another compilation did not even attain publication. An abortive "Cyclopaedia of Universal [or "World"] History" preoccupied Lossing sporadically through the 1880s. In attempting a work on world history, Lossing was approaching a field that was gaining attention from many European scholars. But parochial American readers, some observers thought, had no interest in such studies.[8]

In October 1879, Lossing and Harper & Brothers reached an agreement for the new "Cyclopaedia's" publication. In 1881, Lossing noted that he was "busy on a *Cyclopedia* of Universal history, less minute in detail [than the other compilation] which, if my life and health shall be spared, will be completed, ready for the press, next Fall." He stayed on that schedule, and in April 1882, Harper & Brothers started putting the book in type. Then, suddenly, problems developed.[9]

Harper and Brothers evidently grew concerned that the new compilation might prove as ill-organized as the first *Cyclopaedia*. In December 1882, Lossing felt compelled to offer assurances that "I shall thoroughly *recast*" the new manuscript, adding that "I know I can do it, as I now comprehend the true construction of a Cyclopaedia, from diligent study of the subject." The publisher remained unimpressed and gave Lossing permission to contact other firms. Lossing made such overtures for several years, meanwhile refurbishing his manuscript. In 1884, he remarked in frustration that "I am quietly but very busily engaged in revising my *Cyclopaedia* thoroughly for publication by *somebody*." But "somebody" never materialized.[10]

The "Universal Cyclopaedia's" failure continued the decline of Lossing's connection with Harper & Brothers. Soon Lossing's relations with the firm that had circulated his best books deteriorated even further. After the early 1880s, Lossing seldom corresponded with the publishers. He did produce one more book for them: a dual biography of George Washington's mother (Mary Ball) and wife (Martha Custis). This volume contained a deft narrative and much of the same interest in great forebears' relics as his Mount Vernon work. *Mary and Martha* sold well—just under a thousand copies during two months of 1886, for instance. But to one correspondent Lossing expressed disappointment that his publisher proved so slow at issuing the book.[11] Meanwhile, he looked elsewhere for new opportunities.

Lossing wrote some original biographical works during the 1880s, including several on the American Revolution. Besides the volume about Washington's family, he produced a dual biography of *The Two Spies*: British Major John Andre and patriot Nathan Hale.[12]   Andre, involved in Benedict Arnold's plot to surrender West Point, inspired much interest during the nineteenth century. Circumstances of the militia's capture of Andre and debates over Washington's justification in executing him attracted writers. Antiquarians knew less concerning Hale, so fewer books about him existed.[13]

Lossing developed an interest in Andre by 1850 when, while researching the *Pictorial Field-Book of the Revolution*, he borrowed a manuscript poem the British officer wrote and included a partial facsimile in his work. In the biographical compendium *Our Countrymen*, he noted Andre-Hale parallels.[14]   For a decade before *The Two Spies*, Lossing was involved in discussions of Andre as various groups and individuals considered erecting a monument at his execution's site. He wrote letters to newspapers on this and besides articles on Andre's career.[15]   Meanwhile he began searching for a publisher to handle a topic that he decided could fill a book.

One contact Lossing tried to exploit was Harper & Brothers; he approached them during the 1885-1886 winter. The firm took time to contemplate the offer, taxing Lossing's patience. Late February 1886, found Harper & Brothers still uncertain, although they assured Lossing that "[w]e hope to reach a decision with regard to 'The Two Spies' in a few days." Either that decision proved unfavorable or Lossing grew tired of waiting; in either case, he finally produced the volume for another publisher, D. Appleton & Co., who issued it later that year.[16]

In 1889, Lossing produced a more personal work of Revolutionary biography.   That book, *Hours with the Living Men and Women of the Revolution*, contained embellished versions of interviews Lossing conducted during research on *The Pictorial Field-Book of the Revolution*.[17]   His chatty style in recounting talks with elderly veterans appealed to reviewers, who praised the book. As one remarked, "Dr. Lossing's special mission seems to be to make the dead past live again with a flesh-and-blood reality; and in this new work there is raw material alike for the romancist [sic] and the historian."[18]

Lossing's next major effort was *The Empire State* (1887), a "Compendious History" of New York. This actually represented Lossing's second excursion into his native state's history, since in 1884 he produced a two-volume *History of New York City* that emphasized celebratory biographies of business, intellectual, and social leaders. Both works, especially the volumes on New York City, echoed the combination of optimism and concern over social problems that, a decade earlier, appeared in *American Centenary*. Together they represented Lossing's most ambitious excursions into New

York's history.[19]

Before the 1880s, Lossing wrote about New York's history only briefly, although he planned more extensive projects. In 1872, he described to one correspondent his hopes of visiting Holland and assembling information on early Dutch settlers. This work, he noted, arose "with a view of preparing an illustrated social history of the early times of our great metropolis. I have not abandoned the project—it is only in abeyance." That effort never reached completion, but Lossing maintained contacts with writers involved with such topics. He praised, for instance, Mary L. Booth's *History of New York City*, citing her good treatment of social and political themes that later surfaced in his writings.[20]

In 1881, Lossing tested the waters for a history of the metropolis. He originally contracted with A. S. Barnes and Company for it, but grew convinced that Barnes was not devoting enough energy to publicity. Barnes transferred publication rights to George W. Perine, who worked for them but wanted to establish his own firm. In late 1883, according to one observer, Perine was still "unknown to the [publishing] trade"; but Lossing felt sufficient confidence in him to proceed with the project.[21]

As Lossing conducted research for the work, he stressed the centrality of the biographical sketches that inhabited his footnotes. "The biographies and portraits of men whose character and deeds have done honor to the city of New York illustrate the *history*. Indeed all history is but a record of the actions of men." In assembling the biographical vignettes, Perine and Lossing developed a printed form of "FACTS and DATES" that they sent to likely individuals. One respondent, sculptor John Rogers, felt flattered that Lossing wanted information on his life. "I never received such a compliment before and cannot help feeling that you have made some mistake in asking for a biographical sketch & portrait for your important work." Rogers expressed awe at Lossing's fortitude and erudition. "Such a work as you are engaged in must require an infinite amount of labor to collect all the material but it will be very interesting as all your books are."

In his reply, Lossing noted that Rogers had earlier worked some years in a machine shop; a desire for more details gave him a chance to wax eloquent on the "rags to riches" theme that he found operative in many leaders' careers, including his own. Roger's allusions to that time, Lossing wrote, "give me intimations of the old, old story of the triumph of genius over circumstances, . . . which excites my sympathy and curiosity. Tell me the story . . . of your life as it developed out of a 'machine shop' into the high plane of art to which you have attained. It ought to be known. It is from such evident struggles with circumstances that the greatest benefactors of mankind have issued."[22]

In the *History of New York City*, the first sixty pages presented an outline history to 1830. Within this, the section on seventeenth-century Dutch hegemony offered a generally positive depiction of that period. Lossing admired what he considered egalitarian aspects of Dutch political life that supposedly planted "the germ of representative government in the State of New York." He also liked the honest, unpretentious Dutch settlers' social customs (I: 8, 13). Nostalgia persisted in Lossing's discussion of later periods, although in more modest supply.

After Lossing closed his introduction at 1830, he presented multi-chapter sections on each ensuing decade. In these, Lossing emphasized rapid change and growth in myriad fields of endeavor. By the 1830s, he remarked, the influx of ambitious New England settlers secured "the successful enthronement of an energetic cosmopolitan spirit, which speedily transformed the hitherto quiet, restful, satisfied, and conservative inhabitants of the staid Dutch town into a wide-awake, bustling, elbowing, and ever-restless and aspiring multitude of men and women, scrambling for the headship of every class in the great school of human activity" (I: 66).

From a wider perspective, this sped-up pace had both positive and negative consequences. To its credit, the rise of a diversified economy gave free rein to individual fortitude and enterprise. On the other hand, change encouraged "a strong conviction that social evils were rapidly corrupting public morals and endangering the purity of society," a situation that, in many New Yorkers' minds, required drastic steps toward reform (II: [463], 606). Such remarks revealed Lossing's ambivalence toward nineteenth-century urbanization and uncertainty about whether forces of order and virtue would indeed triumph.

Negative aspects of urban growth grew prominent as Lossing expressed his attitudes toward various ethnic groups. Some new communities won Lossing's praise for accepting Anglo-Saxon norms of behavior and thought. He found New York's Jews, for example, "honest, industrious, and thrifty." His view of Irish immigrants was more troubled. Although he denied sympathy with the nativistic American Party, Lossing criticized the post-1830 growth of Irish political power in the city as a threat to orderly citizens' liberties. Lossing occasionally poked fun at Irish drunkenness and cowardice. But he grew uneasy as he recognized their political power in the hands of "designing demagogues," usually a byword for Democratic machine politicians (I: 125, 244-45; II: 494).

Lossing cited many examples of Democratic exploitation of Irish voters. In the 1834 Election Riots, "[t]here were evidences visible at an early hour . . . that there was a determination on the part of some demagogues to use the brute force of ignorant naturalized citizens, in wards where they largely abounded, in driving the Whigs from the polls." To his credit, Lossing admitted that politicians outside the Democratic Party also proved capable of such tactics—as when the Whigs secured William H. Harrison's presidential victory in 1840. But in most cases demagoguery remained a Tammany Democratic tradition, with the Tweed scandals its natural if unhealthy fruit (I: 314; II: 476, 663, 805).

Happily, Lossing could report that unrest and corruption had not defeated civic-mindedness. Partly from a recognition of growing problems in the social and political realms, many individuals and groups in New York had initiated significant efforts at reform. Early in the nineteenth century, for example, the Provident Society and similar organizations sought to rescue deserving individuals and families from poverty. Such efforts represented "comparatively feeble efforts of large-hearted, broad-minded men and women—the foreshadowings of the magnificent institutions established and carried on vigorously in . . . our day for the same holy purpose"[23]

The success of reform gave Lossing opportunity to conclude on an optimistic note regarding the city's future. This was not to say that no serious problems remained. "The great city, alas . . . presents some of the blackest shadows of social life to be found elsewhere. . . . New York, unfortunately, is becoming in a large degree a city of only two conspicuous classes, the rich and the poor." On a more sanguine note, technology and economic advantages promised New York a future of even greater pre-eminence (II: 865, 866).

Lossing's second effort on New York's history came with *The Empire State*, which, during 1887-1888, went through two editions. It's origins can be traced to suggestions of Horatio Seymour, a past governor, that Lossing compile such a book with illustrations "after the manner of his *Pictorial Field-Book of the Revolution*." Lossing's stated aim in the work was "to embody in one volume, of moderate size and price, a complete outline narrative of the principal events in the career of the Commonwealth . . . so compact . . . that its purchase and perusal will not burden the purses or the leisure of a vast proportion of our people" ([iii]).

The Empire State treated many themes similarly to the *History of New York City*. Lossing's interpretation of Dutch colonization, his anti-Irish propensities, and other themes proved reminiscent of the earlier work. Other topics or approaches were more distinctive or at least gained more extended discussion. To the extent that *The Empire State* contained original ideas, it lay in Lossing's treatment of these subjects.

Discussion of New York's Native Americans recalled allusions in earlier works to a "heroic age" of American history. After mentioning that Dutch settlement began on Manhattan Island, he continued in almost poetic language. "Around the cradle in which the infant empire was rocked stood in wonder and awe representatives of an ancient race, dusky and barbarous in aspect, whose early history is involved in the hopeless obscurity of myth and fable." The Iroquois Confederacy represented "a barbaric republic in the wilderness, simple, pure, and powerful, its capital seated a hundred leagues from the sea, among the beautiful hills and shadowy forests, glittering lakes and sunny savannas, within the present domain of the State of New York" (2).

Meanwhile, despite so many projects, Lossing enjoyed the comforts of his rural home, "the Ridge," near Poughkeepsie. A local history mentioned his estate as having a marvelous view of surrounding countryside. "From his dwelling a fine view is obtained of the mountain ranges of Ulster, Orange, Greene and Sullivan Counties, and of portions of Connecticut." One antiquarian thought that because of its beauty and Lossing's fame, "[t]he 'Ridge' shall always be a landmark in our history."[24]

Such hyperbole notwithstanding, Lossing did enjoy a considerable reputation in these years. In 1882, John Ward Dean, a prominent New England historian, compared Lossing's accomplishments favorably with his own. "Yours has indeed been a busy life and mine has not been an idle one. I hope we may both live many years and make important additions to our literary work. Your fame however [sic] is secure whether you do anything more or not."[25]

Often Lossing's fame encouraged individuals from various walks of life, working from diverse motivations, to approach him with historical queries or desiring his autograph.[26] One correspondent coveted Lossing's views on national prospects, especially whether the historian still thought that the Civil War had solidified republicanism. Lossing's response demonstrated how he retained his faith that the war "was an instrument that purified and strengthened the nation in ever fibre—saved it from threatened invasions—and advanced it in the space of four years, on its way to its destined goal as the dominant political power of the Earth, fully fifty years. This is evinced by the marvellous [sic] development of its resources of every kind and its status in the family of nations."

The nations's stability, Lossing continued, sprang partly from a growing resolve to establish true justice in the treatment of Blacks, Amerindians, and immigrants. It also found expression in civil service reform and in fiscal and diplomatic policies. "In all these things I see the manifestations of divine justice toward the souls and bodies of men, strengthening our people and increasing the power and guaranting [sic] the permanency of the nation."[27] Such perceptions helped to make Lossing's final years comfortable.

Around 1890, Lossing played an obscure role in two surveys of American history. In both cases, the books' publishers approached Lossing about lending his name to ghost-written works which, in theory, he edited and approved. In one case, Lossing probably wrote a chapter on antebellum politics, but he had a small hand in producing other sections.[28] The other book included a portion that Lossing edited, or possibly only read and approved.[29]

The obscurity of Lossing's role in these books suggests something about his status as an author. By this point, Lossing had attained sufficient fame that publishers saw his name on a title-page as a selling point. At the same time, ironically, the editorial process rendered authorship unintelligible. Lossing was famous, but in one sense more anonymous than he had been since his youth. His career had came full circle, and, perhaps appropriately, soon ended.

That end came with hardly a warning. In the 1880s, Lossing and others sometimes grew concerned over his health; but usually things seemed well with him. In 1888, Lossing reported that "I have never been seriously ill in my life, and am as busy at my desk to-day, as ever, thought seventy-five years of age." A friend later remembered that through the spring of 1891 Lossing commented on his "uninterrupted good health[.]"[30] But on June 3 Lossing suddenly died of heart disease at his home near Poughkeepsie. Within days, local newspapers ran obituaries, with New York's printing some especially detailed notices.[31]

Within days, newspapers and magazines throughout the country had printed obituaries of Lossing. One mentioned the coincidence of so many writers dying in 1891, including Lossing, James Parton, and Herman Melville. Several more remarked on Lossing's character as a historian. A Toledo paper called him simply "one of the greatest of modern historians." The Utica *Herald* called Lossing "brilliant, painstaking, indefatigable." Another paper differed mildly, remarking that Lossing's "work was useful rather than brilliant—a conscientious record[.]" Another sheet was more critical. "His accuracy might sometimes be called into question, but his picturesqueness never, and the youth of two generations have delighted in his spirited narratives of great events in the annals of the colonists and of the United States."[32]

When Lossing died, those American journalists who commented on his career were almost unanimous in contending that his work would endure. They stressed the "picturesqueness" of the *Field-Book of the Revolution* as supporting this conclusion. But in the years that followed, awareness of even his best productions practically disappeared, as "local color" increasingly seemed inappropriate for historical writing. In the twentieth century, his reputation rapidly passed into eclipse. Yet for nineteenth-century publishers and readers at various levels of sophistication, Lossing represented a major figure in public historical consciousness. What exactly was his originality and significance as a historian? Why did his fame prove so fleeting?

NOTES

1. Lossing, *Harpers' Popular Cyclopaedia of United States History*. 2 Vols. (New York: Harper & Brothers, 1881); later editions 1882, 1888, 1890, 1892, 1893, 1894, 1895, 1897, 1898, 1898-1899, and, in ten volumes: 1902, 1905, 1907, 1909, 1912, 1915.

2. Memorandum of Agreement, 1 February 1878, Harpers Archives Reel 1, Contract Books Vol. 2, pp. 468-73; Lossing to Samuel G. Arnold, 13 July 1878, Arnold Papers, Virginia Historical Society.

3. J. W. Harper to Lossing, 16 February 1881, LS 805, Lossing Addenda Box 21, Lossing Collection, Huntington Library; Lossing to Harper, 11 February 1881, LS 1338, Ibid.

4. Material with W. D. Alyers [of Harper & Brothers] to Lossing, 20 October 1882, Lossing Collection, Syracuse University Library, Box 2.

5. "Books for the Holidays," *Harper's Weekly* 25 (10 December 1881): 835-[36]; "New Publications," New York *Tribune*, 30 November 1881, p. 6 col. 1. Another review was similar to the *Tribune*'s: "Books and Writers," *Sunday School Times* 24 (7 January 1882): 10-11.

6. "Literature," *The American* 3 (28 January 1882): 251-52.

7. W[illiam] F. Poole, "A Popular Cyclopaedia of United States History," *The Dial* 2 (January 1882): 209-11.

8. "Works on Universal History," *Notes and Queries* 4th s. 8 (9 September 1871): 205-6; "Literary (and Other) Gossip," *The American Bibliopolist* 5 (February and March 1873): [73].

9. Copies of the 28 October 1879 agreement in the Harpers Archives, Reel 2, Contract Books Vol. 4, pp. 45-48, and on Reel 53, Correspondence Relating to Contracts, Box 18. See also Lossing to Lyman C. Draper, 18 March 1881, Draper Correspondence, State Historical Society of Wisconsin, Box 34, and three Lossing to Henry O'Reilley letters in the O'Reilley Collection, Rochester Public Library: 5 January 1880 (item 1240-20); 18 September 1881 (item 1240-31); 5 April 1882 (item 1240-33).

10. Lossing to J. Abner Harper, 25 December 1882, Harper Archives, Reel 53, Correspondence Relating to Contracts, Box 18; Lossing to Charles Gay, 10 April 1884, LS 1353, Lossing Addenda Box 23, Lossing Collection, Huntington Library. See also Gay Brothers & Company to Lossing, 15 December 1883, Lossing Collection, Hayes Library, Box 4; Lossing to Joseph W. Harper, 20 January 1885, Harper Collection, Pierpont Morgan Library.

Manuscripts of the "Universal Cyclopaedia" survived in these collections: Alexander Brown Papers, College of William and Mary, Box 3 folder 59; Lossing Collection, Hayes Library, Box 13; and as LS 7 and LS 286 in the Lossing Collection, Huntington Library.

11. Lossing, *Mary and Martha: The Mother and the Wife of George Washington* (New York: Harper & Brothers, 1886). Lossing to Mr. Adem [?], 15 January 1886, Lossing Collection, Syracuse University Library, Box 3. Data on sales figures appeared in the microfilm edition of the Harpers Archives, Reel 33.

12. Lossing, *The Two Spies: Nathan Hale and John Andre* (New York: D. Appleton and Company, 1886); other editions to 1914.

13. Books on Andre or his captors included: Egbert Benson [Lossing's name-sake], *Vindication of the Captors of Major John Andre* (New-York: Kirk & Mercein, 1817); Jeptha R. Simms, *History of Schoharie County, and Border Wars of New York* (Albany, N.Y.: Munsell & Tanner, 1845); Winthrop Sargent, *The Life and Career of Major John Andre* (Boston: Ticknor and Fields, 1861); Horace W. Smith, *Andreana: . . . History of Major John Andre* (Philadelphia: H. W. Smith, 1865). The topic also inspired some fictional treatments; see especially W. W. Lord, *Andre: A Tragedy in Five Acts* (New York: Charles Scribner, 1856); and D. D. Willsea, "John Andre," *Potter's American Monthly* 14 (March 1880): 174-78, a poem that explicitly related him to Hale. On Hale, see I. W. Stuart, *Life of Captain Nathan Hale, the Martyr Spy of the Revolution* (Hartford, Conn.: F. A. Brown, 1856); also a review in *Putnam's* 7 (May 1856): 476-80.

A discussion of both spies appeared in Samuel Lorenzo Knapp, *Lectures on American Literature* (1829), reprinted as *American Cultural History 1607-1829* (Delmar, N.Y : Scholars' Facsimiles & Reprints, 1977), pp. 254-57.

14. Andre called the poem "The Cow Chace." See also Lossing to [George W.?] Childs, 21 March 1881, in a collector's copy of "The Cow Chace," Clements Library, University of Michigan. Lossing, *Our Countrymen* (New York: Ensign, Bridgman & Fanning; Philadelphia: Lippincott, Grambo & Co., 1855), p. 212.

15. Manuscripts on this involvement included: Dexter H. Walker to Lossing, 18 May 1876; Henry Whittemore to Lossing, 28 December 1878, 30 December 1879, 10 January 1880; all in Lossing Collection, Hayes Library, Box 8. Clippings of newspaper letters were in the same collection, Box 16. See also Lossing, "General Wolfe and Major Andre—A Coincidence," *Sunday School Times* 27 (12 September 1885): 580.

16. Harper & Brothers to Lossing, 20 February 1886, LS 806, Lossing Addenda Box 24, Lossing Collection, Huntington Library.

17. Lossing, *Hours with the Living Men and Women of the Revolution: A Pilgrimage* (New York: Funk & Wagnalls, 1889).

18. "Books and Writers," *Sunday School Times* 31 (29 June 1889): 412-13; see also "New Books and New Editions," *New York Tribune*, 18 April 1889, p. 8 col. 1; unlabeled clipping, 29 June 1889, in Lossing Collection, Hayes Library, Box 4; Funk & Wagnalls press release, Lossing Collection, Hayes Library, Box 20.

19. Lossing, *History of New York City*. 2 Vols. (New York: Geo. W. Perine, 1884); Lossing, *The Empire State: A Compendious History of the Commonwealth of New York* (New York: Funk & Wagnalls, 1887; Hartford: American Publishing Company, 1888). The copy I used was a reprint of the 1888 edition (Spartanburg, S.C.: The Reprint Company, 1968). Following passages owe much to a paper, "Empire State Historian: Benson J. Lossing and Nineteenth-Century New York Historical Writing," Siena Loves New York Conference, Siena College, Loudonville, New York, April 1988.

20. Lossing to Samuel W. Francis, M.D., 27 July 1872; Lossing to Mary L. Booth, 14 June 1880; both in Lossing Collection, Syracuse University Library, Box 3.

21. Lossing to A. S. Barnes & Co., n.d., Lossing Collection, Hayes Library, Box 1; Elie Charlier to Lossing, 9 October 1883, Lossing Collection, Syracuse University Library, Box 2.

22. Lossing to William M. Evarts, 5 December 1882, William Evarts Manuscripts, Yale University, Series II, Box 13, Folder 238; John Rogers to Lossing, 16 September 1882, Lossing Collection, Syracuse University Library, Box 2; Lossing to Rogers, 21 September 1882, Lossing Collection, Syracuse University Library, Box 3.

23. Vol. I: 129. On ideas of reform in this period, see Paul Boyer, *Urban Masses and Moral Order in America, 1820-1920* (Cambridge, Mass.: Harvard University Press, 1978); and Edward K. Spann, *Ideals & Politics: New York Intellectuals and Liberal Democracy, 1820-1880* (Albany: State University of New York Press, 1972).

24. James H. Smith, *History of Duchess County, New York* (Syracuse: D. Mason & Co., 1882), p. 488; typescript of article, Richard F. Maher, "The Old Lossing Homestead," from the *Poughkeepsie Courier*, 10 March 1912, Vassar College Archives. Oddly, this paper's final paragraph spoke of Lossing in the present tense but also referred to his death. The O'Reilley quotation was from his letter to Lossing, 3 April 1882, Item 421d, O'Reilley Papers, Rochester Public Library.

25. Dean to Lossing, 12 April 1882, Lossing Collection, Hayes Library, Box 3.

26. W. L. Mason to Lossing, 28 June 1884, Ibid., Box 6; Lossing to [Mason], 8 July 1884, Ibid., Box 1. A request for an autograph was Maurice L. Madden to Lossing, 27 February 1890, Ibid., Box 6.

27. Lossing to Edgar F. Gladwin, 30 August 1886, Alexander Brown Papers, College of William and Mary, Box 3, folder 54. A slightly different copy of the same letter was in the Lossing Collection, Library of Congress. For an earlier expression of similar views, see Lossing to Samuel Adams Lee, 26 April 1880, Lossing Collection, Hayes Library, Box 1.

28. *The American Nation*, ed. J[ames]. H. Kennedy, (Cleveland: The Williams Publishing Company, 1888-1889). On Kennedy (1849-1934), see *Who Was Who in America* (Chicago: The An. N. Marquis Company, 1943), I: 667.

29. This appeared under several different titles, all from New York's Gay Brothers & Co.: *Our Great Continent; Sketches, Picturesque and Historic: Within and Beyond the States* (1889); *The Achievements of Four Centuries; or, The Wonderful Story of our Great Continent Within and Beyond the States* (1890); *The Countries of the Western World* (1890, 1892, 1893); *The Progress of Four Hundred Years in the Great Republic of the West* (1890).

30. Maria Mitchell to Lossing, 25 April 1886, copy from Vassar College Library in Lossing Collection, Syracuse University Library, Box 4; Lossing to A. H. Markland, 20 February 1888, Park Benjamin Collection, Columbia University; E. H. Goss to Helen R. M. Lossing, 30 July 1891, New York State Library, Call. No. 18107.

31. "Obituary. Benson John Lossing," *New York Times*, 4 June 1891, p. 4 col. 7; "Obituary," *New York Sun*, 4 June 1891, p. 3 col. 4; "Obituary. Benson John Lossing," *New York Daily Tribune*, 4 June 1891, p. 7 col. 5. The *Tribune* obituary served as the basis for "Historian Lossing," *Book News* 9 (July 1891): 449-50.

32. Rochester Chronicle, 16 (?) December 1891, clipping in Lossing Collection, Hayes Library, Box 16; other clippings in Ibid.

10

MORE (OR LESS) THAN
AN HISTORIAN? LOSSING'S
LEGACIES

In the years immediately after his death, Lossing retained a measure of posthumous fame, at least among some publishers and readers. During the following decades, Harper & Brothers and other firms continued to reprint some of his books. The *Cyclopaedia of United States History*, through the efforts of several editors, finally ballooned into a ten-volume work that bore no resemblance to the original but still bore his name. In 1912, New York's War Memorial Association issued extracts from Lossing's *Pictorial History of the Civil War* with Mathew Brady's photographs as illustrations. In 1899, one compilation listed eleven of Lossing's works in print, with Harpers' reissues of the Revolutionary and 1812 *Field-Books* and several school histories dominating the roster. By comparison, Lossing's one-time rival Joel T. Headley, also about a decade past his death, had ten titles available.[1]

Despite this posthumous publication activity, Lossing's reputation quickly declined among academic historical scholars. One reflection of this was how Lossing's writings fared with Albert Bushnell Hart and Edward Channing, Harvard professors and early bibliographers of American history. The 1896 edition of their *Guide to the Study and Reading of American History* cited eight of Lossing's works. Some of these were standard offerings: the Revolutionary and 1812 *Field-Books*, for instance. But Hart and Channing also mentioned less scholarly books, such as *The Two Spies* and the Civil War *Pictorial History*. The 1912 edition dropped the last work because it was too polemic; it also attacked nineteenth-century historians (implicitly including Lossing) for overly stressing military history in their writings: "the details of all warfare are a technical matter, about as instructive to the ordinary reader as the calculation of stresses for bridge building."[2]

Hart made no mention of Lossing in a historiographical paper for the revision of the *Cyclopaedia of United States History*. Despite his disclaimer that he wanted to analyze "tendencies and not [individual] men" among American historians, Hart gave much attention to George Bancroft and Francis Parkman as the most important nineteenth-century figures. He also specified great living historians. But although Lossing originated the medium for Hart's paper, the scholar apparently decided that he did not belong in such company. The nearest Hart came to acknowledging the optimistic perspectives of Lossing was a paragraph on John Fiske, another popularizer of the era.[3]

Why, by a decade after his death, had academic historians lost respect for Lossing's books? Exploring this question is important, first because it allows us to specify his career's impact (or lack of it) on later historical writing. Second, such a discussion can help us distinguish Lossing's character as an historian from that of his more academic counterparts. Our approach must be speculative, because no writers after Lossing's death recorded specifically why he did not deserve their esteem. In addressing this issue, three factors predominate.

First, as an historical investigator Lossing often presented information in ways that academicians found, at best, questionable. The *Field-Book*s contained many citations to original and secondary sources, but even in these works the references often proved oblique or inaccurate. When Lossing wrote hastily or without scholarly pretensions such features disappeared altogether. Even when Lossing wanted to investigate carefully, his inability to organize materials wrecked havoc on his hopes; the *Cyclopaedia of United States History* presented the most glaring example.

Even worse for the new historians, Lossing displayed such a fixation on patriotic themes that the past served mainly as an excuse for his Whiggish moralism. Especially when he wrote about Washington or some similarly sainted figure, Lossing worked from an assumption that leaving their images unsullied represented his just service as a loyal American.

In his review of the *Cyclopaedia of United States History*, William Poole ridiculed Lossing's tendency to repeat hoary myths without questioning their veracity, especially when they seemed poetically fitting or contained useful moral overtones. In fact, sometimes Lossing did explode legends, even in the work that Poole criticized. Although the selectivity of his critical acumen probably resulted from ignorance and not outright deception, Poole and other academicians felt uneasy that Lossing and similar writers could proceed with their works with so little sense of history as a "scientific" enterprise. As Poole remarked in another connection, "[i]t lessens our respect for popular history when myths . . . can so persistently maintain a place in books of American history."[4]

Finally, on an even broader level, Lossing's approach to history was proving unpopular with those who identified with new ideas. One historian has described the history of historical thought in nineteenth-century America as representing a trend away from Providential interpretations and toward stressing history as impersonal process ("historicism").[5] Although open to aspects of evolutionary thought and able to write in such terms, Lossing's sympathies were more with the former approach than the latter. This was something that many academicians could not accept.

Lossing's approach to historical writing was not only proving unfashionable among academicians. It also came to appear dated for many editors, non-academic writers and, as far as we can determine, much of the reading public. Explicating these ideas remains a difficult task, since Americans' discussions of proper approaches to history through the late nineteenth and early twentieth centuries were complex for several reasons. For one thing, commentators varied widely in their definitions of "scientific" and "scholarly" as opposed to "literary" and "popular" historical writing. They also did not agree about what benefits the study of history should bring to writers, readers, or society in general.

Further, distinctions between academic and "popular" historians, although increasingly evident, were still fluid. This was clear when academicians, just beginning to develop their own professional journals, continued writing for literary magazines. With all of these problems in mind, we can still isolate some examples of how academicians and others took various stances on historical writing's proper character and uses.

Contentions that history should employ scientific approaches came from many sources, but an emergent profession of academic historical scholars offered the most important expressions. From its creation in 1884 until after the First World War, the American Historical Association worked from "scientific" views about the historical enterprise, with Herbert Baxter Adams and other leaders insisting that properly trained scholars could reach definitive, objective interpretations that they based upon careful, laboratory-like research. The Association's members paid homage to more traditional scholars, as when they elected George Bancroft one of their first presidents; but the group's dominant tenor was to think of history as a science.[6]

Many observers outside the new profession also argued for scientific historical research and writing. In 1886, a *Harper's* column noted how historians needed to conduct "severe research and investigation, . . . combined with the greatest impartiality[.]" Another commentator made an argument for "logical induction" and empirical research as the necessary means for saving history from myth-making. "Delight in any kind of falsehood is always wrong." A teacher concluded a paper on "Methods of Teaching General History" with the observation that "in history as in science truth and strength can be reached only by bringing children face to face with . . . real things[.]" Another essayist granted that scientific history often proved dull reading, but saw such works as necessary foundations for "that interpretation of human life which is in itself a contribution toward the perfecting of life."[7]

Such views persisted into the early twentieth century. One writer claimed to find history far different from literature, since "while literature is primarily a matter of feeling, history is primarily a matter of knowledge." H. Morse Stephens, a Cornell professor, noted that "[i]t is now recognized that the aim of the scientific and conscientious historian should be to discover and to state simply and truly what has happened in the past. . . . It is his duty to be objective rather than subjective[.]" But Stephens also granted that such a perspective "has hardly yet penetrated into the consciousness of the intelligent majority of the reading public. Brilliant but inaccurate narratives are still too often considered good histories[.]"[8]

On the other hand, perceptions of "scientific" historiography as unnecessary or unwelcome also appeared through these years. A speaker before one historical society claimed that, because all of American history unfolded within the age of printing, mythologizing was no threat to investigators. "We are not compelled to resort to tradition or fancy to eke out authoritative records." In words Lossing would have endorsed, a textbook's writer contended that poetry was a good source for history because "[n]othing . . . will aid more in fixing a fact of history in the memory of a boy or girl than a stirring ballad or poem, in which the fact or incident is pictured before them with all the charms of imagination." *The Nation* attacked scientific historians for pedantry.[9]

Some observers who enjoyed good reputations among academic scholars also wanted to retain literary distinction in historical writing. Naval scholar Alfred T. Mahan weighed scientific history in a balance with literary approaches and found the former wanting. "The old-fashioned historian thought it a point of honor to write in a style at once lucid and picturesque. The modern is too generally content to throw his material into an unshapely mass[.]"

In a similar way, President Theodore Roosevelt poked fun at scientific scholars as "all of the conscientious[,] industrious, painstaking little pedants, who would have been useful people in a rather small way if they had understood their own limitations, [but] had become because of their conceit distinctly noxious." Another writer argued that historians were already returning to a more literary ethos. "The assumption that the historical monograph, being a 'scientific' product, might be put together regardless of form, has been fully tested, and has broken down."[10]

Still others criticized both the scientific and literary paradigms as, in themselves, only partly right. A *Sunday School Times* columnist noted how, because of scholars' work, the concept of "tradition" now possessed both positive and negative connotations. Aware of such complexity, that writer did not make any pretense of reaching a definitive judgment about the status of historical knowledge. Justin Winsor argued in the *Atlantic* that the scientific school's claims to objectivity were attractive but untenable because causation was so difficult for even the best scholars to establish.[11]

With all these competing viewpoints operative, perceptions on Lossing and similar nineteenth-century historians fell across a wide range. Hart and others agreed that his most serious contributions deserved respect. But the larger proportion of Lossing's books seemed beneath contempt. In such books, Lossing's style and even his approach to history had passed out of fashion. Many "latter-day historians" had rejected nineteenth-century attitudes that successful historical writing must employ "dramatic" or "picturesque" language, or that history could buttress theology by presenting events in a Providential light.

Arguably this statement merely begs the most important question: why had historians' tastes changed so profoundly within a generation? For one reason, nineteenth-century models no longer appeared adequate as historiography sought academic respectability. History, many scholars thought, needed more consistent analytical rigor than earlier writers were able or willing to bring to their work. In this view, Lossing, whatever his admitted talents for lucid writing, seemed distinctively less than a true historian.

Beyond any doubt, such views contained some validity. Lossing never held consistent ideals of scholarly exactitude, and many of his books sprang as much from commercial motives as from concern to further readers' knowledge about American history. Even during his lifetime, scholars critiqued his approach as too concerned with maintaining readers' comfortable perspectives on the national past and optimism about the future.

But in another sense, the idea of distinguishing among such values as patriotism, commercial success, and factual accuracy would not have occurred to Lossing. He acted from an assurance that he could serve all those aims at once. Indeed, for Lossing, a truly successful work was one that buttressed love of country, recorded events accurately, and turned a profit. The uneven course of his life revealed that he experienced difficulty in realizing these goals, but that never led him to doubt their attainability or mutually supporting character. Whether consciously or by implication, many later historians rejected Lossing's perspective and renounced his motivations. But for an understanding of nineteenth-century American uses of history, his long career held sufficient importance to render him, at least in some commentators' view, "more than a historian."

Was serving as a reflection of once powerful ideas Lossing's only significance? Beyond recognizing that views he expressed were popular in his time but later proved unacceptable for most historians, can a study of his long and busy career teach us anything regarding, as this study's introduction suggested, "the history of historical thought in American culture"? This chapter's conclusion will posit some tentative answers based upon widely differing potential interpretations of Lossing's career.[12]

First, to approach our theme in a negative light, one might argue that, since his fame proved transitory, Lossing was ultimately a failure in his attempts to write popular and edifying history. One could say Lossing even failed during his lifetime, given his perpetual activity that won so few commercial rewards. This failure, and the patriotic interpretations readers associated with it, perhaps fostered cynicism among Americans regarding history's lessons, making it seem pointless and hence marginalizing the influence of later historians.

The way in which history soon became mainly the preserve of academic writers, far from negating this marginalization, possibly demonstrates it, since many readers rejected the new scholars' visions of history along with earlier interpretations. Academic history secured many accomplishments in the century after Lossing's death, and its intellectual sophistication proved formidable; but its practitioners tended to write for each other, seldom reaching wider publics. They sought to write better history than Lossing and others like him by disclaiming commercial aims; in the process, history became increasingly irrelevant to American culture.

Second, in a more positive sense, it is possible that Lossing and writers like him did not fail, despite their fall from public consciousness. As this chapter has shown, the scientific historiography that displaced Lossing and similar writers never enjoyed unanimous favor, even among academicians. In the twentieth century, various trends demonstrated that the scientific viewpoint would itself fall as scholars attacked the objectivistic assumptions which served as the foundations for scientism in historical research and writing.

As it became influential after the First World War, Progresive historiography jettisoned earlier scholars' ideas that history could and should be objective and refrain from taking sides in political or social issues. For the Progressives, history always possessed a strong component of activism, representing something scholars and political leaders should use in the interest of reform. In their hands, history ceased to be a value-free discipline and began, for the first time since Lossing's era, to take on moralistic overtones. The specifics of those overtones were far different than those of writers fifty years before, and those differences were important. But from a broader perspective, one could argue that the return of moralistic history of any type recreated earlier traditions in historical writing.[13]

These traditions persist in contemporary American thought, finding particular expression in two very different ways of approaching history. First, in some circles of evangelical Protestantism, recent writers have made a rediscovery of Providential interpretations of American history. This has had practically no impact among even consciously Christian scholars, but its popularity among non-academic audiences suggests that such interpretations continue to fulfill spiritual and intellectual needs for many Americans, and that these ideas influence political and social mores in profound ways.[14]

The wider scholarly community reflects even more vividly the idea that discovering and making political, social, and moral applications is a large part (perhaps the most crucial part) of the interpretative process in historical scholarship. This is not a proper place for a detailed treatment of how, especially in the last generation, historians and other scholars have "politicized" their fields by making political and social relationships basic to their paradigms for understanding history. It is important that controversies over "political correctness" typically have more to do with specifics of how one interprets history to make political statements than whether making such interpretations is a legitimate enterprise. Many historians of our time, academic and non-academic alike, from a variety of political, social, and religious backgrounds, agree that their views on history reflect their larger perspectives on the world and that their discipline can never have much utility if it claims a value-free status.

In an ironic way, Lossing and other historical popularizers of his time would have felt quite at home in this environment, conditioned as they were by careers of making history a tool for political debate and social commentary. One might conclude, therefore, that Lossing's writings remain a mirror for our times as well as for his. Specifics of his worldview continue to attract many Americans, searching, as people always have, for a world that makes sense. Even for those who, out of the same instinct, reject his understanding of events, his larger goal of tracing America's past in order to influence its present and future remains a compelling and challenging ideal.

NOTES

1.   *The United States Catalog: Books in Print, 1899*, ed. Marion E. Potter and George Flavel Danforth (Minneapolis: H. W. Wilson [et. al.]: 1900), pp. 293, 398.

2. Channing and Hart, *Guide to the Study and Reading of American History* (Boston: Ginn, 1896); Channing, Hart and Turner, *Guide* Rev. and Augmented ed. (Boston [et. al.]: Ginn and Company, 1912), p. 10.

3. Hart, "The American School of Historical Writers," in *Harper's Encyclopaedia of United States History*. 10 Vols. (New York, London: Harper & Brothers, 1902), xxvii-[xlvii]; quotation and last reference from p. xlv.

4. Poole, "The Persistence of Historic Myths," *Dial* 11 (October 1890): [143]-46; quotation from p. 146.

5. Dorothy Ross, "Historical Consciousness in Nineteenth-Century America," *American Historical Review* 69 (October 1984): 909-28.

6. On the rise of an American academic historical profession see W[illiam] Stull Holt, *Historical Scholarship in the United States and Other Essays* (Seattle and London: University of Washington Press, 1967), pp. 3-63; H[ugh] Hale Bellot, *American History and American Historians* (Norman, Okla.: University of Oklahoma Press, 1952), pp. [1]-40; the early chapters of John Higham, *History: Professional Scholarship in America* (Baltimore: Johns Hopkins University Press, 1983); and Peter Novick, *That Noble*

Dream: The "Objectivity Question" and the American Historical Profession (Cambridge, England [et al.]: Cambridge University Press, 1988).   On the trend toward professionalization in the late-nineteenth century and early-twentieth century, see Burton J. Bledstein, *The Culture of Professionalism: The Middle Class and the Development of Higher Education in America* (New York: W. W. Norton & Co., 1976); Mary O. Furner, *Advocacy & Objectivity: A Crisis in the Professionalization of American Social Science, 1865-1905* (Lexington, Ky.: The University of Kentucky Press for the Organization of American Historians, 1975); Thomas L. Haskell, *The Emergence of Professional Social Science: The American Social Science Association and the Nineteenth-Century Crisis of Authority* (Urbana, Ill.: University of Illinois Press, 1977).

7. "Literary Notes," *Harper's* 72 (January 1886) reprinted in *Harper's Lost Reviews,* comp. Clayton L. Eichelberger (Millwood, N.Y.: KTO Press, 1976), p. 1; see also "Literary Notes," *Harper's,* Ibid. (April 1886) in *Harper's Lost Reviews,* Ibid., p. 15; Susan Channing, "The Historical Method," *The Writer* 1 (November 1887): 163-64; quotations from p. 164; Mary Sheldon Barnes, "Methods of Teaching General History," in National Education Association, *Journal of Proceedings and Addresses, Session of the Year 1891, Held at Toronto, Ontario* (St. Paul, Minn.: Published by the Association, 1891), pp. 673-77; quotations from p. 677; "The Historical Spirit," *Atlantic* 73 (March 1894): 409-14; quotation from p. 412.   For similar ideas from earlier decades, see [J. A. Froude], "The Science of History," *Hours at Home* 2 (February 1866): 321-30; William Swinton, "The New Lamps of History," *The Galaxy* 10 (July 1870): 97-108.

8. Frederic Austin Ogg, "On the Literary Decline of History," *Dial* 32 (1 April 1902): 233-35; quotation from p. 234; H. Morse Stephens, "Some Living American Historians," *The World's Work* 4 (July 1902): 2,316-27; quotations from pp. 2,316, 2,319.

9. Charles H. Bell, *Discourse Delivered Before the New-England Historic, Genealogical Society, Boston, March 18, 1871* (Boston: New-England Historic, Genealogical Society, 1871), p. 20; T. F. Donnelly, *Primary History of the United States* (New York: A. S. Barnes & Company, 1885), p. vi.; "History and Literature," *Nation* 71 (25 October 1900): 325-26; "A New Intrusion of Pedantry," *Nation* 77 (24 December 1903): 498-99.

10. A. T. Mahan, "The Writing of History," *Atlantic* 91 (March 1903): [289]-98; quotation from p. 293; Roosevelt quoted in Theodore S. Hamerow, *Reflections on History and Historians* (Madison, Wisc.: The University of Wisconsin Press, 1987), p. 54; William Roscoe Thayer, "The Outlook in History," *Atlantic* 96 (July 1905): 65-78; quotation from p. 69.

11. "Notes on Open Letters," *Sunday School Times* 31 (6 July 1889): 418-19; Justin Winsor, "The Perils of Historical Narrative," *Atlantic* (September 1890): [289]-97. One nonscholarly observer thought that historians could merge literary insight with scientific rigor: Emma W. Rogers, "The New Writing of History," *Methodist Review* 87 [5th s. 21] (January 1905): 44-52.

12. Much of the material in the following paragraphs reflects my reading of Novick, *That Noble Dream.*

13. Richard Hofstadter, *The Progressive Historians: Turner, Beard, Parrington* (Chicago: University of Chicago Press, 1968).

14. I have in mind such books as Peter Marshall and David Manuel, *The Light and the Glory* (Tarrytown, N.Y.: Fleming H. Revell Company, 1977).

BIBLIOGRAPHIC ESSAY

A concern to offer specific comments, especially on primary materials, encouraged me to develop a bibliographic essay rather than a more conventional listing of sources. Here I will not repeat sources on the theory and methodology of cultural history, which I enumerated in the notes of Chapter 1, or on the history of historical writing in the United States, for which I refer readers to notes in Chapters 1 and 10. My goal in the following comments is to help readers evaluate materials I used in Chapters 2 through 9, the passages that concentrated directly on Lossing's career.

MANUSCRIPTS

The largest and most significant collection of primary sources on Lossing resides at the Henry B. Huntington Library in San Marino, California. Besides approximately forty boxes of correspondence and family or financial records, this includes manuscripts of several books, notebooks from Lossing's research travels, and hundreds of pencil and ink sketches. The Huntington Library also holds materials on Lossing in its Robert Brock and Francis Lieber collections. The Lossing Collection at the Rutherford B. Hayes Library in Fremont, Ohio, is nearly as large as the Huntington's, and, besides rich correspondence, contains large files of newspaper clippings.

Other manuscript collections on Lossing are smaller than those of the Huntington and Hayes libraries, but still proved important in my research. The Vassar College Library has several boxes that naturally contain information on Lossing's involvement with that institution, but much else as well. Syracuse University has three boxes of manuscripts and another box of duplicates from Vassar. In New York City, the New York Public Library and the New-York Historical Society contain significant holdings, as does the Detroit Public Library's Burton Historical Collection and the Historical Society of Pennsylvania.

In a third group of repositories, I found smaller but useful Lossing Collections or relevant materials in other collections. Among these, I should mention the Adriance Memorial Library in Poughkeepsie; the American Antiquarian Society; the Clements Library at the University of Michigan, Ann Arbor; Columbia University; the Perkins Library at Duke University; the Pierpont Morgan Library; the Southern Historical Collection at the University of North Carolina, Chapel Hill; the University of Virginia; the Swam Library at the College of William and Mary; the Virginia Historical Society; the Mount Vernon Library; the Rochester (New York) Public Library; and the State Historical Society of Wisconsin's Lyman C. Draper Collection.

Finally, I should mention repositories, most of which I did not personally visit, whose staffs kindly supplied me with copies of manuscript or printed material on Lossing. These included: the Bancroft Library at the University of California, Berkeley; the Minnesota Historical Society; Knox College; the Indiana Historical Society; the Western Reserve Historical Society, Cleveland; Oberlin College; the Filson Club, Louisville; Dickinson College; the University of Rochester; Cornell University; Hamilton College in Clinton, New York; the Brooklyn Historical Society; the University of West Virginia; the Library of Congress Manuscript Division; the University of South Carolina; and libraries at Princeton, Yale, Brown, and Harvard.

NEWSPAPERS

Besides clippings in manuscript collections, I consulted microfilm editions of many newspapers to locate Lossing's writings or trace events in his life. I read the Poughkeepsie *Telegraph* at the Adriance Memorial Library and the Poughkeepsie *Daily Eagle* at the Vassar College Library. When references in manuscripts or indexes suggested that articles relating to Lossing or historical writing appeared, I read various papers, mostly from New York City. The New York *Times* proved the most important for my purposes. Two religious papers, *The Sunday School Times* and *The Independent*, not only contained some of Lossing's essays but many thoughtful book reviews.

BIOGRAPHICAL SOURCES: GENERAL

Two nineteenth-century collective biographical works on American writers contained information on Lossing and many other historical writers. George and Evert Duyckinck, *Cyclopaedia of American Literature*. 2 Vols. (New York: Charles Scribner, 1856) had detailed narratives of individuals' lives, but usually only polite evaluations of their books. S. Austin Allibone,

A Critical Dictionary of English Literature and British and American Authors Living and Deceased. 3 Vols. (Philadelphia: J.. B. Lippincott & Co., 1882) offered briefer entries but many quotations from scholarly and popular reviews. Among later works, the *Dictionary of American Biography* proved invaluable, as did some volumes of Gale Research Company's *Dictionary of Literary Biography*.

BIOGRAPHICAL SOURCES: LOSSING

Besides the entries on Lossing in sources I just cited and in some of the more detailed book reviews, the best source that predated his death was "Benson J. Lossing," *Appleton's Journal* 8 (20 July 1872): 69-71. Nathaniel Paine, *A Biographical Sketch of Benson J. Lossing* (Worcester, Mass.: Privately Printed, 1892) was worshipful but informative; both qualities adhered in lesser degree to Mary L. D. Ferris, "Benson J. Lossing, LL.D.," *American Author* 1 (May 1902): 101-5.

Later commentators have brought more scholarly exactitude to treatments of Lossing. David D. Van Tassel, "Benson J. Lossing: Pen and Pencil Historian," *American Quarterly* 6 (Spring 1954): 32-44, remains a good treatment of the broad contours of Lossing's career; J. Tracy Power, "Benson J. Lossing," in *American Historians, 1607-1865*, ed. Clyde N. Wilson, Vol. 30 of *Dictionary of Literary Biography* (Detroit: Gale Research Company, 1984), pp. 163-68 is also helpful.

For Alexander Davidson, "How Benson J. Lossing Wrote His Pictorial Field-Books of the Revolution, and War of 1812 and the Civil War," *Papers of the Bibliographical Society of America* 32 (1938): 57-64, the article's title reveals its more limited aims, as does Diane M. Casey, "Benson Lossing: His Life and Work, 1830-1860," *Syracuse University Associates Courier* 20 (Spring 1985): 81-95, which makes good use of manuscripts at Syracuse University.

LOSSING'S WRITINGS

I found original, reprint, or microfilm editions of most of Lossing's books at the University of Wisconsin-Madison's Memorial Library and the Library at the State Historical Society of Wisconsin. The Historical Society's Manuscript Department also had a set of *The Family Magazine* that included the volumes Lossing edited. I own a reprint of the 1860 edition of *Pictorial Field-Book of the Revolution*, which I compared with earlier editions.

INDEX

About the Author

HAROLD E. MAHAN is Professor of American Studies at Minnesota Bible College.

ISBN 0-313-28806-2

90000>

EAN

9 780313 288067

HARDCOVER BAR CODE